CARING FOR THE HIGH MOUNTAINS

- *Conservation of the Cairngorms* -

Edited by
J.W.H. Conroy
Adam Watson
A.R. Gunson

ISBN. 0 906265 13 4

COVER. **The Summit of Cairn Gorm from Ben Macdui.** *The wide expanse of the plateau in summer, home to the snow bunting and dotterel. (Nick Picozzi)*

CARING FOR THE HIGH MOUNTAINS
PROCEEDINGS OF THE CONFERENCE
ON CONSERVATION OF THE CAIRNGORMS

UNIVERSITY OF ABERDEEN 12 March 1988
edited by J.W.H. Conroy, Adam Watson and A.R. Gunson

CONTENTS

SESSION ONE

SESSION TWO

INVITED PAPERS

DESMOND NETHERSOLE-THOMPSON
1908-1989

Desmond Nethersole Thompson (Right) with editor Adam Watson
(Photograph by Chris Lowell)

This volume is dedicated to the memory of Desmond Nethersole-Thompson, who died in March 1989 at the age of nearly 81.

His contribution to ornithology in the Cairngorms was outstanding and he believed strongly in the need for better conservation of this magnificent area.

He did much on behalf of the people of the Cairngorms, as Inverness-shire County Councillor for Rothiemurchus for nearly 20 years and as Chairman of Badenoch District Council 1952-55.

INTRODUCTION

Within the European Community, the Cairngorms are the most important area for subarctic-oceanic mountains, moorland and boreal forest and home to wildlife of international importance. They offer a wide range of opportunities for outdoor recreation, shooting, fishing, study (in particular for children to understand how these mountains were built and to experience their natural history), and for visitors to come and view this beautiful land. The demands from many of these activities have led to increased pressure on the area, be it for additional downhill skiing facilities, bulldozed tracks, car parks etc. Over the past forty years, intensive afforestation has also encroached into the mountainous areas. For many years now there have been growing demands both nationally and internationally for this part of the Cairngorms to be given adequate protection.

The Cairngorms, however, extend beyond the mountains into the valleys, the villages, estates and farms. The area's rich human culture and history are of great interest and linked to the mountains.

The Cairngorms are therefore an interaction of their people and the land. These need not, and should not, be looked upon as separate. What occurs in one part can often affect others. Because of these increased pressures there is now a need to try and find the best methods for meeting the various demands on the area, while still maintaining the integrity of the area's more important parts, and the identity of its local cultures.

It was with this aim in mind that the Institute of Terrestrial Ecology (ITE) and the Centre for Scottish Studies at the University of Aberdeen hosted the Conference *Caring for the High Mountains – Conservation of the Cairngorms* in March 1988. Speakers were invited to present cases for conservation, development and management of the area as a whole, to look beyond the main Cairngorms massif, particularly the National Nature Reserve and its immediate environs, to the wider area around it. In addition to those presented at the Conference, papers for the Proceedings were requested and received from the Regional Planning Authorities and the Countryside Commission for Scotland.

The result is this volume, which we hope will help increase people's awareness of the uniqueness of the Cairngorms environment, the problems involved in managing it and the need for a rational approach to solving them. The Conference offered no simple answers and passed no resolutions. These are best expressed by individuals and organisations involved in the area. Since the Conference, the Scottish Office has invited the Countryside

Commission for Scotland to examine ways of protecting Scotland's popular mountain areas including the Cairngorms. Their report is expected during 1990.

We thank those who gave papers to the Conference and the Proceedings, especially the Rt Hon Alick Buchanan-Smith MP, who changed a busy schedule to open the meeting, the students who helped run the Conference, and the typists at the Institute and University who typed the papers.

Grateful acknowledgement is also given to Grampian Regional Council, Angus District Council, Gordon District Council, Kincardine & Deeside District Council, Moray District Council, the Nature Conservancy Council, the Highlands and Islands Development Board and Mobil North Sea Ltd. for financial assistance towards the cost of publishing the proceedings.

J.W.H. Conroy
Adam Watson
A.R. Gunson (*Editors*)
June 1989

FOREWORD

THE RT HON ALICK BUCHANAN-SMITH M.P.
House of Commons, London SW1A 0AA

I welcome the opportunity of writing the foreword to this book of the Proceedings of the Conference on *Caring for the High Mountains – Conservation of the Cairngorms* which I had the privilege of opening in March 1988. Our heritage in the Cairngorms is very precious and we are right to be concerned about it.

There is a real danger of growing conflict between those who wish development, whether for downhill skiing, other sports, or forestry, and those who wish more emphasis on conservation.

I hope we avoid unnecessary conflict, because conflict can result in people becoming entrenched in their views, unwilling to listen to arguments and consequently is unlikely to lead to good decisions.

To take the example of downhill ski development on Cairn Gorm, those who support its expansion point out that the present development covers 1.25 per cent of the Cairngorms National Scenic Area (Cramond this book), that downhill skiing is a good and popular sport in which nine per cent of Scottish adults participate, and how much better for people to enjoy themselves in the mountains in a participatory sport than be stuck, for example, on the terracing of a football ground in a city.

Those who oppose expansion could in the past justifiably point to rusting machinery, to broken turf and heather, soil erosion, and sometimes ineffective attempts to repair the damage to the surface of the ground.

Fortunately, the latter picture is, I believe, improving. New developments, such as Glas Maol at Glenshee have been much more carefully planned and controlled. There the material was flown in by helicopter, and care taken with excavation and construction and the removal of spoil. The result is a minimum of physical damage and visual impact.

After discussions with a wide range of interested parties from both the voluntary and statutory sectors, Management Plans, incorporating many of the points raised, have been drawn up for the operations at Glenshee and the Lecht. Both the Glenshee Chairlift Company Ltd and the Lecht Ski Company Ltd employ, as a matter of course, professional ecologists to undertake annual monitoring of the effects of current skiing.

Sensible commercial development should ensure financial ability to comply with such plans. This indicates what reasonable planning, cooperation and responsibility can achieve.

When discussing downhill ski developments, one tends to forget that the conservation/recreation lobby are not, in general opposed to them. Rather they see the need for an overall strategy for ski development in a Scottish context. Even on Cairn Gorm, the opposition is only for developments west of the existing facilities across the Northern Corries and into Lurcher's Gully, an area designated by the Nature Conservancy Council as a Site of Special Scientific Interest (SSSI) in 1984. Further planning applications for development here will, I fear, once again lead to conflict between interested parties.

I hope that we can proceed by consensus and compromise. I know these are not the most popular words today, particularly in political circles: nonetheless, if this can be achieved, it should offer the most constructive chance of progress. In several recent developments at the Lecht, Glenshee and the new proposal for Drumochter this has occurred. There has been the potential for conflict between the development and conservation interests (the developments encroaching into SSSIs or a National Nature Reserve). In each instance, the Nature Conservancy Council, as the statutory body responsible for conservation, objected (as on occasion did other groups). A compromise was reached, the conservation argument was not upheld, the development permitted, but the planning conditions attached to the development went some way to safeguard the conservation interests.

In some areas, however, there must also be support to protect areas of national and international importance against development, regardless of their size or the advantages of these areas for development.

If this results in policies and practices being achieved by agreement, they are much more likely to stick and be effective in the long term, rather than mechanical regulation.

There is still more to be done. I believe there is scope for more independent research to be undertaken.
For example:

a. in ski areas, is the damage all done by skiers, or is it the foot of man that does most damage to the high plateau, assisted by easy access from ski lifts?

b. what are the effects of human disturbance on birds?

c. studies on regeneration; this is important if we wish to preserve the Old Caledonian forest;

d. what are the implications of pollution such as acid precipitation and black snow?

I am hesitant whether particular designations of an area – such as a National

Park – will necessarily achieve our ends, but what is needed is some overall management plan for the area. In this, I welcome Grampian Regional Council's attempt to produce such a plan for the Eastern Cairngorms (Grampian Regional Council this book).

Understanding of the issues by the different viewpoints has progressed and, altogether, I sense a more positive and constructive approach. We certainly must avoid polarisation of views – that has been and would continue to be disastrous.

I would point out that this is not just a Cairngorms problem. It arises elsewhere in Scotland and Britain, and I have also witnessed it myself in the Alps. And I understand it extends beyond Europe to the Himalayas. In seeking a policy for the Cairngorms, we are part of a far wider process. Let's hope we succeed. It is vital that we look after and husband our unique physical environment.

CHAIRMAN'S OPENING REMARKS

THE CAIRNGORMS

R. BALHARRY

Chief Warden, Nature Conservancy Council,
Wynne-Edwards House, 17 Rubislaw Terrace, Aberdeen AB1 1XE

The Cairngorms are a special place, for both wildlife and people. Here is a tract of high summit plateaux and corries, of deep glens, and fast flowing rivers. The Cairngorms are a place where the visitor can gain an insight into the functions of the natural world or be inspired by the beauty, wildness and sheer wonder of the surroundings.

Shepherds, stalkers, farmers and foresters earn their living by managing the renewable natural resources. The tourist industry is sustained by the scenic grandeur with which the area is so well endowed. Communities survive and thrive in the scattered townships and villages. All are dependent on one another.

The core of the area is, however, remote and devoid of human habitation. The hills of Ben Macdui, Braeriach, Cairn Toul and Cairn Gorm all rise above the 1200 metres level. This is unique habitat – the largest area of land at this elevation in the British Isles. It is home for the dotterel and snow bunting, and a goal for people with strength in limb, curiosity of spirit and unquenchable enthusiasm.

The conference was convened to discuss today's land use issues, examine management improvements and explore means of safeguarding this priceless heritage for tomorrow.

Defining the boundaries of the Cairngorms as a complete ecological unit is a difficult task but for the purposes of the conference we are using the area chosen by the Scottish Development Department (SDD) in 1967 (Scottish Development Department 1967). Roughly circular in shape, it includes land in Highland, Grampian and Tayside regions and six districts; all, along with landowners, have a say in the management of the area. From east to west it covers approximately eighty kilometres and north to south seventy kilometres, encompassing close on 4050 square kilometres. (Map 1).

The purpose of the SDD's 1967 report was to study the problems and possibilities of this area. Today, the problems and concerns are still with us. Reconciling the different interests of land use, of development and nature conservation is at the heart of the debate.

In July 1954 when the Cairngorm Natural Nature Reserve (NNR) was declared, the then Director General of the Nature Conservancy, Max Nicholson, said:

> We do not want the area opened up to charabancs and helicopters, and whatever future horrors there may be .....! It is time therefore more was done about instructing the ordinary citizen in the elements of Natural History so that he may respect his obligations as well as his rights when he gets into the country side. The problem has not been neglected altogether, yet present efforts to resolve it inspire little confidence (Nicholson 1954).

The environmental, social and economic issues are complex. The importance of the area for its scientific, cultural, educational, inspirational and aesthetic qualities is often underestimated or inadequately understood. Determining policies for future management is not easy. It has been said that conservation is a compromise between that which is a biological necessity and that which is politically expedient.

In 1982 large parts of the Cairngorms were listed by the International Union for the Conservation of Nature and National Resources (IUCN) as a natural site under the designation of a World Heritage Site (IUCN 1982). The criteria needed for such a listing are impressive:

> That it be of superlative natural beauty. A site that illustrates significant geological processes and natural habitats crucial to the survival of threatened plants and animals. These sites ensure that maintenance of the natural diversity upon which all mankind depends.

The British government have not confirmed this designation. This is more fully discussed in these proceedings (Curry-Lindahl this book).

The Cairngorms are not only an important and invaluable part of our Scottish heritage; they are the heritage of all mankind. The papers of the conference are given by leading and eminent figures on the interests of nature conservation, development, landowning, forestry and recreation.

REFERENCES

IUCN 1982. *The World's Greatest National Areas.* IUCN, Gland, Switzerland.

NICHOLSON, E.M. 1954. Report in *Glasgow Herald* (9 July 1954).

SCOTTISH DEVELOPMENT DEPARTMENT (1967). *Cairngorm Area.* HMSO, Edinburgh.

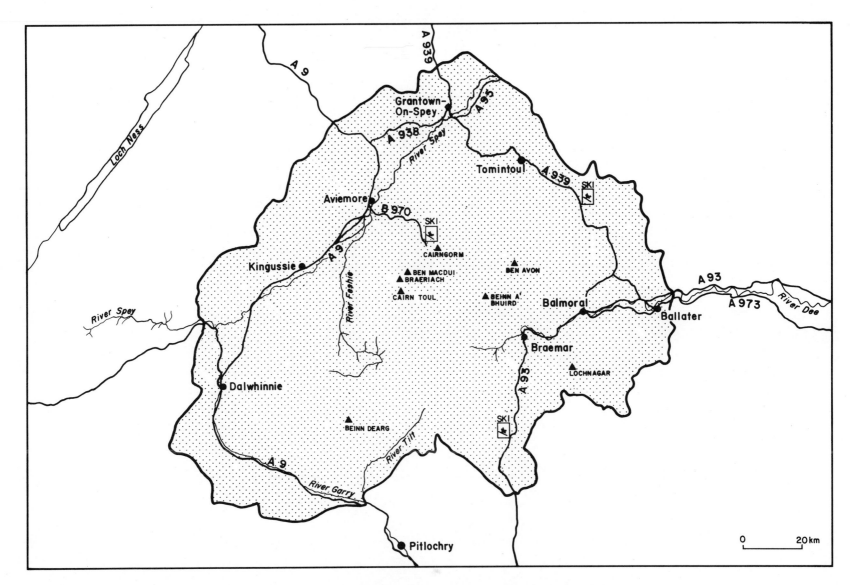

Map 1. The boundaries of the Cairngorms after SDD (1967).

CAIRNGORM – CONSERVATION AND DEVELOPMENT: LIVING TOGETHER

R.D. CRAMOND

Deputy Chairman, The Highlands and Islands Development Board, Bridge House, Bank Street, Inverness

INTRODUCTION

The Highlands and Islands Development Board's (HIDB) Cairngorm Estate forms a small, but important, part of the Cairngorms, whose international significance for conservation is widely acknowledged (Ratcliffe 1977, see also this book) not least by the owners of this small part of the massif. The Board's ownership of the Estate dates from the early 1970s. Following a decision by the Forestry Commission that the upper slopes of Cairn Gorm were not required for afforestation, the then Secretary of State for Scotland decided that the Board should acquire the land for the controlled and proper development of winter sports in the area, and for the proper maintenance of the Estate. The major form of development has been the provision of additional facilities for downhill skiing by the Cairngorm Chairlift Company Ltd (the Company) which leases 844 hectares of the total area of 2350 hectares from the Board. The Estate, however, is also used for a variety of other activities, both winter and summer, ranging from grazing reindeer to rock climbing, hill walking, cross country skiing and scientific research.

DOWNHILL SKIING

In terms of Scottish downhill skiing centres, Cairn Gorm is the largest with over half the total number of skier days – 362 000 skier days in winter 1986/87 (Mackay Consultants 1988a). Cairn Gorm skiing puts about £10 million into the local economy each year, creating the equivalent of some 280 direct full-time jobs, and up to 2000 indirect and part-time jobs during the ski season. (Mackay Consultants 1986). Demand for Scottish downhill skiing has been growing at an average rate of at least five per cent per annum in the last few years, and present facilities at Cairn Gorm are seriously overstretched.

TABLE 1

The area leased for downhill skiing at Cairn Gorm in relation to other areas nearby

The Cairngorms National Scenic Area (which includes Cairngorm Estate)	67 400 hectares
The adjacent Cairngorm National Nature Reserve	26 000 hectares
Leased area as a percentage of the National Scenic Area	1.25%
Leased area as a percentage in relation to the National Nature Reserve	3.25%

Table 1 sets the area leased for downhill skiing on the Board's Estate in its wider geographical context. The Royal Society for the Protection of Birds (RSPB) has recently purchased the Abernethy Forest Lodge Estate. This covers 8500 hectares, about ten times the size of the downhill skiing area on Cairn Gorm. The total area of land encompassed by the four main downhill skiing areas in Scotland, taken together, is 2150 hectares. This would fit four times over into the Abernethy Estate.

This is not implying criticism of the size of the National Nature Reserve (NNR) nor of the size of the Abernethy Reserve. On the contrary I welcome the RSPB's purchase and look forward to working with them. I am simply asking people to be aware that downhill skiing developments occupy a relatively small area, compared with other land uses in the Cairngorms.

Some people believe that the Secretary of State's decision after the 1981 Lurcher's Gully Public Inquiry meant that there should be no further downhill skiing developments in that area. However, the Lurcher's Gully Public Inquiry was about a specific planning application by the Cairngorm Chairlift Company Ltd which envisaged a comprehensive skiing development across the three Northern Corries, including chairlifts and ski tows, and, importantly, a public access road and car parking facilities in the corries (Scottish Development Department 1982a).

In his decision letter, the Secretary of State, while agreeing with the Reporter that the site of the proposed development was of outstanding scientific, scenic and recreational importance, said that he did not intend his decision *in that particular case:*

to rule out the possibility that a more limited scheme for additional facilities at Cairn Gorm, which required no road extension beyond the existing car park, might represent an acceptable balance between development and conservation objectives.

That decision letter also announced the Government's intention to draw up notes and guidance on the location of winter sports development as part of the National Planning Guidelines in order to reduce the further scope for conflict between downhill skiing development proposals and other forms of land use (Scottish Development Department 1982b).

The *National Planning Guidelines for Skiing Developments* (Scottish Development Department 1984) recognise Cairn Gorm as a primary area for further downhill skiing development, and state that the improvement and expansion of facilities there should be a priority aim. The difficulties being experienced by local development groups in bringing forward new skiing developments elsewhere in Scotland also underline the need for additional capacity at Cairn Gorm.

The Nature Conservancy Council (NCC) then notified its intention to make the whole of the Northern Corries a Site of Special Scientific Interest (SSSI). The HIDB and Highland Regional Council opposed this. The Board commissioned an independent scientific assessment of the area. This was carried out for us by ASH Consultants (Anderson Semens Houston 1984).

The NCC notification said, *inter alia,* that the Northern Corries formed an integral part of the internationally important Cairngorm Mountains, and that the variety of physical and biological features which they contained made them the most valuable of all the arctic cliff corries within the Cairngorm Mountains. The citation went on to describe the variety of ground and the changes in altitude from Rothiemurchus and Glenmore Forests to the summit of Cairn Lochan. It further stated that the lower slopes were predominantly of heather, whilst some of the best cliff and scree flora was to be found higher up on the cliff buttresses and gullies. Attention was drawn to the arctic vegetation on the upper slopes. Importantly, the citation noted that, as a result of a reduction in grazing by red deer, native Scots pine and juniper were becoming established on the high moorland, creating a sub-alpine scrub zone. Indeed, that was true, and part of the reason that the red deer no longer graze may well be the presence of the skiing development (Miller 1986).

The assessment carried out by ASH Consultants concluded that the geomorphic and botanic features of the site were not unique to the Northern Corries. They said that similar natural conditions and geomorphic interest occurred elsewhere in the Cairngorms, and that a particularly fine assemblage was to be found in the area of Braeriach, which is itself within the Cairngorms National Nature Reserve. They further pointed out that the site was not of uniform scientific interest, and the report indicated parts which could be termed of significant, moderate and low interest. They also reported that the scientific interest was mainly on the upper basins and slopes of the corries and the corrie headwalls, and that, whether the site was designated or not, this could be at risk in the long term from unmanaged use by climbers, hill walkers and teaching uses of the site, and from continual grazing pressure from sheep.

Overall, the report concluded that, although certain features justified part of the site being designated as an SSSI, the fact remained that the scientific interest (although not the accessibility) was duplicated, and in many respects was inferior to, for example, the adjacent Braeriach area. The review team concluded that the site was being proposed as an SSSI, not because of its own scientific merit, but as an extension to the Cairngorm Grade 1 site, and as a buffer to the NNR.

The NCC rejected this evidence but assured us that SSSI designation would not necessarily prevent development. The Board offered to sell to the NCC the land above the 910 metre contour in the area of Coire an t-Sneachda and Coire an Lochain, which included the cliff flora. The NCC did not accept this offer. They said:

> Given that NCC is currently reviewing its policies for conservation of the whole of the Cairngorms NNR/SSSI, the Committee (the Scottish Advisory Committee) did not feel that it was appropriate at this time to negotiate for the area on offer.

That was in February 1985. It is not known whether that review has been completed, but the offer to sell remains.

Some people also claim that further development in the Northern Corries was ruled out by the Government following the Scottish Affairs Committee's investigation of the Board, part of whose Report dealt with the Cairngorm Estate (Scottish Affairs Committee 1985). That is not so. The Government's reply to the Committee's Report was that the National Planning Guidelines for Skiing Developments provided the framework within which skiing development on Cairn Gorm could be considered. They drew attention to the fact that the Guidelines recommended that there should be further skiing development on Cairn Gorm, subject to consideration of access, and consultation with interested parties. They went on to say that it was for the HIDB to decide how far and in what ways it should assist the development of skiing in these areas, in the light of its priorities and the resources available.

In 1986, the Government backed up that view by deciding not to call in an application by the Cairngorm Chairlift Company Ltd for planning permission to erect snow fences in Coire an t-Sneachda and to allow Highland Regional Council itself to deal with the application. In his decision letter, the Secretary of State accepted that the continued success of the ski operations at Cairn Gorm was important to the local economy, and that the proposed development was desirable to improve the quality of skiing at Cairn Gorm. He noted that the corrie concerned was already used by skiers in favourable conditions, that the visual impactof the new fencing would be small, and the impact on the vegetation in the corrie would be limited – indeed, that the most important plant communities were located in parts of the SSSI which would not be affected by that development. He also drew attention to the fact that the proposed development was fully in line with the National Planning Guidelines. The snow fences concerned have been erected in conformity with the stringent planning conditions imposed by the Regional Council. The Company itself carried out an environmental impact assessment as part of its planning application.

MANAGEMENT OF THE CAIRN GORM ESTATE

So much for development. What about management? We have produced a comprehensive Management Plan for the Cairngorm Estate (Highland and Islands Development Board 1987), against the background of the substantial growth in the use of the Estate in recent years, not only by downhill skiers, but by walkers, climbers, naturalists, researchers and other groups enjoying informal recreation in a splendid environment.

Up until this time, the Board's management of the Estate had been undertaken by staff in consultation with its two neighbouring tenants – the Cairngorm Chairlift Company Ltd and the Reindeer Company. In practice, and indeed in terms of their lease, a large number of the day-to-day management tasks have been undertaken by the Cairngorm Chairlift Company. Overall management has been achieved principally through our own staff and the Cairngorm Ranger Service which is run by the Company on behalf of the Board. The broad basis of this management approach was based on a survey by Land Use Consultants (1972). That work led us to produce objectives and policies for the management of the Estate. However, by the early 1980s, it was clear that the vast increase in public use of the Estate, and potential further development, required us to update our Plan substantially. We therefore produced this revised Management Plan. I would emphasise that an updated Management Plan was required whether or not any further development took place on the Estate.

The Plan, published in summer 1987, is essentially in three parts – first, a detailed description of the Estate and the management issues; second, the policies to be followed in managing the Estate; and third, the prescriptive actions to implement these policies. An important aspect of the Plan is the management of visitors. This is a difficult and delicate task and sensitive means will have to be employed to encourage at least most people to keep to established paths and to avoid the most sensitive areas for the flora and fauna. We envisage a minimal amount of direct management techniques, but we will expect the experienced countryside users to respect the environment and the neighbouring National Nature Reserve.

The Plan also envisages the network of roads, paths and tracks being kept to the minimum required to cater for the different users. Any new facilities provided on the Estate will have to be constructed and maintained after paying attention to the handbook *Environmental Design of Ski Areas in Scotland* produced for the Countryside Commission for Scotland (CCS) and Highland Regional Council (ASH Environmental Design Partnership 1986).

Management of visitors is the key issue, and before effective management can take place more information is required about the patterns of use of the Estate. The Board therefore joined with the Highland Regional Council, the Nature Conservancy Council and the Countryside Commission for Scotland and commissioned a Summer Visitors Survey (Mackay Consultants 1988b). The report makes interesting reading. Estimates from traffic counters on the Cairn Gorm road and at the Linn of Dee (Deeside) indicate that some 150-175 000 visits were made to the Cairngorms NNR and Estate during July, August and September. It is difficult to compare directly, but some comparisons with an NCC survey carried out in 1973 suggest that summer visitor numbers have probably increased by about forty per cent.

The most striking feature of the survey results is the wide diversity of visitors and activities pursued in the area. Of particular interest to the Board is that traffic counts recorded 115 382 visits to the Coire Cas car park during the survey period, i.e. sixty per cent of the total visits to the area. Loch an Eilein accounted for another 25 000 visits. The patterns of activity at these two localities are very different from other locations, and affect only a small proportion of the total area. At Coire Cas, around twenty five per cent of visitors left their cars for only a few minutes, and over sixty per cent spent less than two hours there. Just over a fifth went up the chairlift. Perhaps the most striking finding related to visitor attitudes towards the area of the NNR and Estate combined. Ninety-two percent said they would return, implying a high degree of satisfaction. Of interest, some seventy five per cent thought the area had either improved or not changed in recent years. Visitors mentioned improved and additional facilities, improved access and improved management as positive factors; whereas increasing visitor numbers, commercialisation, erosion and man-made changes were mentioned as negative features.

What we now have to decide are effective ways of managing, in particular, the substantial number of visitors who use the chairlifts in summer. As the Management Plan for the Cairngorm Estate pointed out, the easy access to higher altitudes means that Cairn Gorm provides a unique opportunity for many to experience a mountain environment. We therefore accept the use of the chairlifts by sightseers, scientists and casual walkers in summer as a legitimate one. Equally, it is recognised that the primary land use within the National Nature Reserve is nature conservation, and that recreational and other uses can conflict with this.

More is therefore needed to be known about the extent of damage and disturbance to the environment, and it is necessary to find ways of managing visitors which will minimise their intrusion into the National Nature Reserve. This will obviously have to be done in close consultation with the NCC and the RSPB, whose land occupies the area of the National Nature Reserve closest to the summit of Cairn Gorm. Action here will have to be co-ordinated, and this makes it urgent for the NCC and the RSPB to produce their own Management Plans for the NNR and the adjacent Upper Glen Avon and Abernethy Estates.

With the conclusion of the Summer Visitor Survey, it has now been decided by all the bodies concerned to carry out similar work over the 1987/88 winter and thereby gain valuable information about the numbers and types of people who use the Estate for informal recreation over the winter months.

Another piece of worthwhile research being carried out and grant-aided by the Cairngorm Chairlift Company in conjunction with the CCS, NCC and the Board is a study of snow buntings from late 1987 onwards by Mr Richard Smith. The snow bunting, a rare bird at the southernmost edge of its breeding range, is using the increased food opportunities provided by skiing developments. Whilst large flocks of this Arctic migrant are common over much of Scotland in winter, fewer than twenty pairs breed in Scotland in most years. This current research should put the impact of ski centres on snow buntings into perspective.

There is also an ongoing programme of repairs to the Northern Corries' footpath. This started in 1986 and continued in 1987, and it is planned to do more in 1988, provided that NCC's approval is given. Properly designed and constructed paths will have less visual impact than areas of eroded ground or haphazard networks of paths and we strongly believe that properly maintained paths, which will minimise the area of ground disturbed, are much preferable to allowing them to evolve in a haphazard way.

The task of improving the Northern Corries' path is associated with the monitoring work being carried out by the Cairngorm Ranger Service into the condition of the path and the number of people using it. Better liaison with the Army has now been established, and arrangements agreed with them to control strictly the numbers of Services personnel using the Estate. Guidance is given about environmentally sensitive areas so that they can be avoided in recreation and training activities.

We have also discussed with the CCS and NCC the possibility of additional tree planting on the Estate but, on their advice, have decided not to proceed with it.

For the past two years we have employed a shepherd – in fact, in 1986 it was a shepherdess – to prevent sheep from neighbouring areas straying onto our land and destroying patches which had been carefully reseeded. That work will be repeated on an annual basis until such time as there is no danger of the sheep being hefted to the hill. In this connection it is interesting to note that a recent inspection report by Watson (1988) found that damage in summer 1987 to the recently developed slopes of Glas Maol and Fionn Choire at Glenshee was mainly being caused by sheep, not skiers or piste machines. He found that sheep usage had been concentrated by snow fencing and the sheep had done a lot of damage to re-seeded patches within the fenced areas. That squares with our experience at Cairn Gorm.

A great deal of attention has also been given by the Board and the Cairngorm Chairlift Company to improving the rehabilitation of bare ground, including the use of reseeding techniques. Further work on this is being assisted by a study of soil erosion by Dr Adam Watson in summer 1988 with financial assistance by CCS, NCC and the Board. We are also joining with the Commission in a study on the restoration of upland vegetation; a piece of work which will be done by the Institute of Terrestrial Ecology (ITE). In 1987 the Cairngorm Chairlift Company Ltd purchased a sophisticated machine called a Hydroseeder. This should greatly assist the Company in its annual programme of reseeding. In this, expert advice has been taken about the seed mixture used, and it is now supplemented by an organic fertiliser.

In the foreword to the Management Plan (Highlands and Islands Development Board 1987), the point was made that the Board's Estate does not exist in isolation, and that it is part of a much larger area of outstanding scenic attraction – indeed the whole Cairngorms' massif. That makes it essential that the work we do in implementing the Plan is co-ordinated with the owners and tenants of the surrounding estates, and of course with the Government agencies most closely concerned – the NCC and the CCS. We need the understanding and help of all concerned and, acting on a recommendation in the Plan, it is our intention to establish a monitoring/ advisory group on an informal basis, whose task it will be to provide us with advice as the Plan is progressively implemented. We really should welcome constructive help.

VISITOR PRESSURES AND THE 'HONEY POT' IDEA

These are some of the detailed management considerations for the Estate. We are faced with an intractable problem – very similar to that faced by the National Trust for Scotland and others who own beautiful and environmentally sensitive areas which people want to visit. Visitor pressure is there, will not go away and will in fact increase as more and more people have leisure and as more and more people are encouraged by advertisements, television holiday programmes and wildlife programmes to visit such areas.

Nor should we try to stop them. Members of the public have a right to enjoy Scotland's scenery and to share the special magic of areas like Cairn Gorm. It is better to say 'Come this way', rather than 'No Entry'. In other words, visitor pressures have to be managed in ways which will minimise damage to fragile environments. This is not easy, but there is something to be said for the 'Honey Pot' technique. The great thing about downhill skiers, for example, is that they stick very close to the uplift facilities and so you can have 7000 of them in a very small area. The point is that, sadly, there is going to be some damage somewhere because of sheer visitor numbers. But if visitors can be channelled to one relatively limited area where paths can be provided that is surely better than letting damage spread haphazardly over much wider areas.

The National Trust for Scotland had a similar problem at Ben Lawers, and have been criticised for building a visitor centre and a car park on that hillside and so attracting more people to see the alpine plants. But the visitors at least are channelled on to particular paths, to which most adhere. Moreover, the visitor centre explains the value of the plants and so educates people – it is hoped – into leaving them alone. Moreover, it reduces the possibility of people going to another area where there are equally valuable alpine flowers, which are left in peace because very few people know about them. Similarly, the RSPB have done a great job at Loch Garten by providing facilities for large numbers of people to watch ospreys. But they rightly conceal the locations of the very many other sites where ospreys are now breeding in the Highlands.

Again, the Countryside Commission for Scotland has been criticised for making long-distance footpaths. But, if the increasing numbers of people who want to walk in our countryside are given access to areas where they know they can walk without risking challenge, then the very many truly wild areas of Scotland can be left for those who have the strength, the skill and expertise to reach them, without paths, and to experience complete solitude.

Moreover, those who say that it should not be made easy for people to get access to any wild or high areas are forgetting the claims of the old, the disabled and the parents of young children. Surely these groups of people are entitled to have relatively easy access to at least a few high places. I count myself now as one of these. At one time I could walk and climb in Glencoe, Skye, Torridon, the Dolomites and even the Himalaya. With a plastic hip, it is not so easy. Yet I would like occasionally to revisit one or two of the high or remote places that I used to enjoy so much.

I am not suggesting that much of Scotland be traversed by long-distance footpaths, nor that every beautiful mountain should have a car park, a visitor centre and a chairlift. I am saying that if we provide a relatively few such facilities, then the visitor pressure will be transferred to them, leaving the vast bulk of Scotland for those who do not want, do not need, or actively despise such facilities. So let's have mutual tolerance. There surely is room for walkers, climbers, orienteers, skiers, ornithologists, botanists, geologists and all other kinds of '– ists' in Scotland.

In particular, let us not exaggerate the extent of provision for downhill skiing in Scotland. I am not a skier and never have been, but I do not understand why so many other mountain users object to ski developments. If one does not wish to look at uplift facilities, then most of Scotland, and even ninety nine per cent of the Cairngorms massif, is available. If you want the wilderness experience, then don't come to the HIDB Cairngorm Estate. Go to Morven or Moidart or Morar or Knoydart or Applecross or Torridon or Coigach or Assynt or northwest Sutherland (to name but a few). Even go west from Aviemore instead of east, or go over the back of Cairn Gorm where, within a mile or two of the chairlifts, total solitude can be experienced.

I am particularly glad to hear that the RSPB are going to encourage people to visit their large new reserve at Abernethy. It alone is ten times the size of the skiing area at Cairn Gorm. It can surely absorb many visitors without damage.

FUTURE SKI DEVELOPMENT ON THE CAIRN GORM ESTATE

This brings me now to the question of the further development of downhill skiing on the Estate. In the Introduction, I referred to the growing demand for skiing. The Cairngorm Chairlift Company has produced a Development Plan for the 1980s and 1990s (Cairngorm Chairlift Company Ltd 1986) which has been subject to intense scrutiny by a Working Group set up by the Highland Regional Council, whose members included the NCC, CCS, the Cairngorm Chairlift Company and the Board, under the direction of the Director of Planning (Cairngorm Development Plan Working Group 1987). All the members of that working group concluded that demand for skiing at Cairn Gorm is expected to continue to increase, whether or not development takes place at other existing and proposed new skiing centres. I think that is important because all on the Working Group accept that over-crowding on Cairn Gorm will not go away by spreading skiing to new developments elsewhere.

Another important conclusion of the Working Group was to agree that the Company should do everything practicable to consolidate skiing within the eastern skiing area on the mountain, but that even then such consolidation would only ease, but not solve, the growing pressure of demand. The Working Group also saw a real danger that unless capacity is increased, dissatisfaction with Cairn Gorm as a major skiing area will grow and diminish the reputation of Scottish skiing as a whole.

What of the proposed developments themselves? Apart from the representatives of the NCC, the Working Group members concluded that expansion to the west into Lurcher's Gully was a feasible proposition. They decided that the visual impact of a carefully sited skiing development could be limited to a localised area, and would not detract from the views from the plateau or from Loch Morlich and the A9. Again, apart from the NCC officials, the Working Group were of the opinion that the key landforms and rare plant communities of the Northern Corries SSSI should not be impaired by a carefully sited and managed skiing development.

We now come to the crunch issue! How do the skiers get into Lurcher's Gully? As you can imagine, that question occupied a great deal of the Working Group's thinking. They looked at a ski tow, a chairlift, a rack railway and a shuttle bus access road. At the end they thought that the road was preferable because not only would it be more operationally sound, but it would have the least visual and environmental impact along the route. The Working Group did, of course, recognise the argument that a well-surfaced road or track, even if closed to vehicles apart from the shuttle bus, might increase access to the NNR in summer. There was also an argument that a road west of the present Coire Cas car park would be contrary to the National Planning Guidelines, but there I would argue that the Planning Guidelines were drawn up in the context of the Lurcher's Gully Public Inquiry into the proposal which envisaged a public road and car parks in the gully. However, as the Working Group recognised, the interpretation of the Guidelines is a matter for the Secretary of State. Highland Regional Council's road engineers have made an examination of possible routes for a shuttle bus access road, and have concluded that the best line for this would not only be the least environmentally sensitive, but would also be the cheapest. However, we should not get too carried away about the question of a road, because the Working Group also concluded that a cableway would be equally feasible and probably not that much more expensive, if at all. I would have thought that, from the NCC's point of view, concerned as they are about the possibility of increased access to the NNR, a cableway would be preferable as it could be shut down completely outside the skiing season.

The recommendations of the Working Party were accepted by the Regional Council and have been incorporated in their revised draft structure Plan (Highland Regional Council 1988) and the Badenoch and Strathspey Local Plan.

In the meantime, the Chairlift Company has proceeded with consolidation measures in the east. They have:

    a. introduced snow fencing to maximise use of the existing snow fields;

    b. rationalised the snow fencing in lower Coire Cas;

    c. installed a Telekit Poma tow in Coire na Ciste.

Further measures are being considered as part of the framework plan suggested by the Working Group for development and consolidation in the east and expansion in the west. It seems, therefore, that before too long the issue of planning consent for development of Lurcher's Gully will once more be to the fore. It is also clear that any such planning proposal will be fiercely contested by the NCC and others. Personally, I regret this very much because all concerned on the development side have, over the past seven years or so, gone out of their way to demonstrate that a great deal of time and money has been, and will be, spent on measures to minimise damage to the environment, in its broadest sense, including the flora and fauna, the geomorphological features and the scenery.

From the developers' point of view, it has now been conclusively demonstrated that development in the west is viable operationally and financially, and would make minimum calls on the public purse. Indeed, the Cairngorm Chairlift Company Ltd have a successful financial track record over the past twenty years, even taking into account those years when snow has been in short supply. I am confident that they will be in a position to finance developments in the west mainly from their own financial resources. This is very important because the National Planning Guidelines make a special point that new downhill skiing facilities should make a minimum call on public expenditure.

After giving full weight to the environmental and other features of the Northern Corries which need to be preserved and looked after, it is surely best in national terms to maximise further skiing development in places which are already highly developed and where the extension can be carried out simply and without further substantial calls on public funds. Surely, also, it must make sense to enable development to take place on one of the very few places in the Highlands, and indeed in Scotland, where downhill skiing can prosper. I have already shown that the area of land taken up by all skiing developments in Scotland is very small. There are hundreds of thousands of acres of hill and mountain land in Scotland – widely dispersed over the whole country – which can cater for the environmental, recreational and other informal sporting activities of those who feel that their enjoyment of their particular interest on Cairn Gorm is harmed by downhill skiing developments.

The best potential slopes for downhill skiing in Britain are on Braeriach. It is, however, also of high conservation interest, and all of us are determined that Braeriach must be preserved for conservation. So development cannot go there. If there were other suitable areas which were less scientifically interesting than is Lurcher's Gully, and equally good for skiing, then the Company would go to them, but the fact remains that there are no such areas. The Cairngorm Chairlift Company have given the firm assurance that if they were permitted to develop uplift facilities in Lurcher's Gully then, from their point of view, that will be their limit. From the HIDB's point of view, whatever happens – and whether there is further development or not – I can confirm that a high measure of priority, and the staff and money needed, will be devoted to looking after the Estate because we recognise how highly important it is as part of our upland heritage.

Cairn Gorm is precious in scenic and environmental terms – but one per cent of it is also the 'jewel in the crown' of Scottish downhill skiing. As such it contributes greatly to the economic and social health of part of our area and gives enjoyment and recreation to many thousands of people in Scotland and elsewhere. Would those who enjoy walking and climbing in our hills deny to skiers the very small part of them where downhill skiing development is possible?

CONCLUSION

We as one small landowner in this area have a very difficult task and would welcome the co-operation of other landowners, and of interested statutory and voluntary agencies, in reconciling competing pressures, achieving better understanding between groups of users, and operating the Estate in the interests of the whole people of Scotland and many others from other countries.

No doubt criticism will continue from some quarters, but I hope that all will accept that we are genuinely trying to do our best, in very difficult circumstances, to cope with competing pressures. It is easy to criticise what others are doing – and no doubt I shall indulge in that luxury myself after I retire – but when one actually has the responsibility, as owner, of trying to cater for competing pressures on a small area of land, one realises how difficult it is. It is easy to make headlines: but difficult to devise constructive solutions, so I am pleading for greater understanding, greater communication,greater mutual tolerance, greater realisation that there are no easy answers. As I said earlier, visitor pressure will not go away; it will increase. All landowners in the area, including ourselves, have to try to produce means of coping with and channelling these pressures so that they do minimum damage to a sensitive area. No-one has a monopoly of love of beautiful and wild areas, and no-one should have a monopoly of access to them. I ask everyone who is concerned about these areas to help those who have the responsibility for managing them and for trying to provide for and reconcile the public pressures upon them.

REFERENCES

ANDERSON SEMENS HOUSTON (1984). *A Review of the Case for the SSSI Designation of the Northern Corries Area of Cairngorm.* (A Report to the Highlands and Islands Development Board). ASH Environmental Design Partnership, Glasgow.

ASH ENVIRONMENTAL DESIGN PARTNERSHIP (1986). *Environmental Design of Ski Areas in Scotland. A Practical Handbook.* Report for the Countryside Commission for Scotland and Highland Regional Council. ASH Environmental Design Partnership, Glasgow.

CAIRNGORM CHAIRLIFT COMPANY LTD. (1986). *Development Plan for the 1980s and 1990s.* Cairngorm Chairlift Company Ltd., Inverness.

CAIRNGORM DEVELOPMENT PLAN WORKING GROUP (1987). *Advisory Team's Report and Responses.* Highland Regional Council Planning Department, Inverness.

HIGHLANDS AND ISLANDS DEVELOPMENT BOARD (1987). *Cairngorm Estate Management Plan.* Highlands and Islands Development Board, Inverness.

HIGHLAND REGIONAL COUNCIL (1988). *Highland Region Structure Plan Review 1988* (Consultation Draft). Highland Regional Council, Inverness.

LAND USE CONSULTANTS (1972). *Highland and Islands Development Board Cairngorm Estate Survey.* (A Report to the Highlands and Islands Development Board).

MACKAY CONSULTANTS (1986). *Expenditure of Skiers at Cairngorm and Glencoe.* Highland and Islands Development Board, Inverness.

MACKAY CONSULTANTS (1988a). *The Future Development of the Scottish Skiing Industry.* Scottish Development Agency, Edinburgh.

MACKAY CONSULTANTS (1988b). *Cairngorm Visitor Survey Summer 1987.* (A report for the Countryside Commission for Scotland, Highland and Islands Development Board, Highland Regional Council and Nature Conservancy Council) Mackay Consultants, Inverness.

MILLER, G.R. (1986). *Development of Subalpine Scrub at Northern Corries, Cairngorms SSSI.* Institute of Terrestrial Ecology, Banchory.

RATCLIFFE, D.A. (1977). *A Nature Conservation Review.* Cambridge University Press, Cambridge. (2 vols.)

SCOTTISH AFFAIRS COMMITTEE (1985). *Second Report Session 1984-85. Highlands and Islands Development Board.* HMSO, London.

SCOTTISH DEVELOPMENT DEPARTMENT (1982a). *Findings of the Lurcher's Gully Public Inquiry, Kingussie.* Scottish Development Department, Edinburgh.

SCOTTISH DEVELOPMENT DEPARTMENT (1982b). *Lurcher's Gully Public Inquiry – Decision Letter.* Scottish Development Department, Edinburgh.

SCOTTISH DEVELOPMENT DEPARTMENT (1984). *National Planning Guidelines for Skiing Developments.* Scottish Development Department, Edinburgh.

WATSON, A. (1988). *Environmental Baseline Study – Glenshee Ski Centre 1987.* Institute of Terrestrial Ecology, Banchory.

*EDITORIAL NOTE: Since the Conference, CCS have on balance recommended against the development of downhill skiing facilities in Lurcher's Gully (COUNTRYSIDE COMMISSION FOR SCOTLAND (1989). *Westward Expansion of Skiing at Cairngorm.* Countryside Commission for Scotland, Perth).

THE ROLE OF THE NATURE CONSERVANCY COUNCIL IN PROTECTING THE CAIRNGORMS

E.M. MATTHEW

Regional Officer, NE Scotland, Nature Conservancy Council, Wynne-Edwards House, 17 Rubislaw Terrace, Aberdeen AB1 1XE

INTRODUCTION

"The Cairngorms are regarded as the most important mountain system in the country and of international importance for nature conservation". This is the opinion of the Nature Conservancy Council (NCC) as expressed in the Nature Conservation Review (NCR) by Ratcliffe (1977).

Official interest in the conservation of the Cairngorms began in the 1940s and was first manifest with the publication of the report of the Scottish National Parks Committee in 1947 (HMSO 1947). The Cairngorms were one of five areas in Scotland recommended in the report as National Parks. In 1949 the Scottish Wildlife Conservation Committee proposed that the high ground above 770 metres in the Cairngorms should be made a National Nature Reserve. In 1954, less than five years after Britain's official wildlife agency, the Nature Conservancy, was established, the Cairngorms National Nature Reserve (NNR) was declared. Covering 16 060 hectares, it was the largest Nature Reserve in Britain (Map 1). Declarations in 1962 and 1966 enlarged the Reserve to its present size of 25 950 hectares. The NCC owns only twelve per cent of the Reserve, eight per cent is owned by the Royal Society for the Protection of Birds (RSPB) and the remainder is in private hands. Together with the RSPB sector these areas are managed under Nature Reserve Agreements with NCC. The Cairngorms have thus been protected by National Nature Reserve status for thirty-four years. The most important parts of the wider Cairngorms area have been notified as Sites of Special Scientific Interest (SSSI). These include the Eastern Cairngorms (1971), Northern Corries (1984) and Rothiemurchus Pinewood (1988) immediately adjacent to the Cairngorms NNR. Under the Wildlife and Countryside Act (1981), NNRs must also be notified as SSSIs. The Cairngorms NNR was notified in 1987. This SSSI includes extensions beyond the Reserve boundary in Rothiemurchus, Mar and Glen Feshie (Map 1). Details of the Nature Conservancy and NCC management plans can be found in the references (Nature Conservancy 1959, 1968; Nature Conservancy Council 1985, 1987).

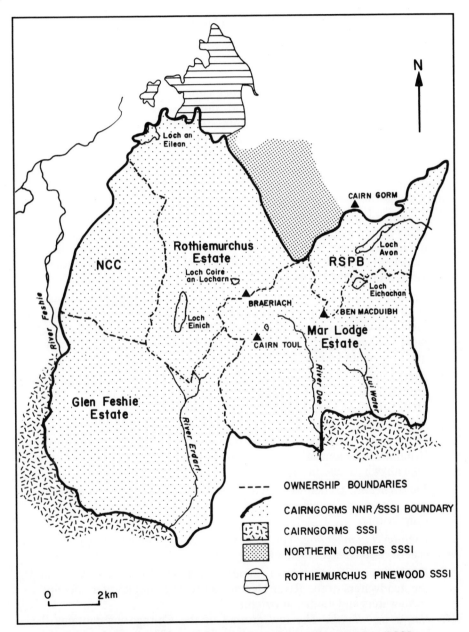

Map 1. Ownership of the Cairngorms NNR, with adjoining SSSIs.

VALUES OF THE CAIRNGORMS

The Countryside Commission for Scotland (CCS) has designated the Cairngorms as a National Scenic Area (Countryside Commission for Scotland 1978). The Cairngorms are also of national importance for outdoor recreation, hill walking, winter and rock climbing, ski touring and natural history studies. On the other hand their values for sport shooting, commercial forestry and grazing by domestic stock are limited by their poor soils, high altitude and exposure. The Nature Conservancy Council regards the upland habitats, native woodlands and arctic-alpine lochs of the Cairngorms as of international importance for nature conservation (Ratcliffe 1977). The constituent parts of the wildlife and landform values of the Cairngorms make up a catalogue of superlatives.

1. *Large size.* Features of nature conservation value have usually been badly fragmented in Britain. Large size is therefore a valued attribute in nature conservation. The juxtaposition of large areas of native forest, moorland and high plateaux extending over a wide range of altitudes is a key feature of the Cairngorms.

2. *Natural condition.* Large areas are in a near-natural condition and are evolving with little interference from man. The landscape of Britain is highly modified and areas in a near natural condition are scarce and highly valued. The Cairngorms are probably the least man-modified extensive inland area in Britain.

3. *Arctic quality.* The Cairngorms contain by far the largest area of high ground in Britain. This ground is the nearest equivalent in Britain to the arctic tundra and supports a unique fauna and flora.

4. *Summit heaths and snow beds.* There is a much greater extent and range of variation of summit heaths and snow beds than anywhere else in Britain. The extent of *Juncus trifidus* heath is greater in the Cairngorms than anywhere else in the world.

5. *Lichen heaths.* Lichen-rich heaths are confined to ground with an eastern distribution in Britain. Some of the best examples are found in the Cairngorms.

6. *High-level blanket bog.* The highest large area of blanket bog in Britain is at over 900 metres on the Moine Mhor.

7. *Fresh waters.* The high-level corrie lochs, Lochs Einich and Avon, and the headwaters of the River Dee are outlying examples of arctic-alpine fresh waters and unique in Britain.

8. *Native woodlands.* The low ground of the Cairngorms contains the largest native woodland remnants in Britain. They are dominated by

Scots pine, the most local native woodland type in Britain. They support a specialised northern boreal fauna and flora. The only fragment of a natural altitudinal treeline in Britain is found in the Cairngorms.

9. *Arctic-alpine flora*. The Cairngorms are an important regional refuge for arctic-alpine flora.

10. *Fauna*. The fauna of the Cairngorms is characteristic of northern forests and mountain environments and includes a large number of rare species. The rare nesting birds of the area are an outstanding attraction. Thirty-two species of insect, the second largest score for any site in Scotland, are listed in the Red Data Book (Shirt 1987), which shows rare, endemic, endangered and vulnerable species.

11. *Flora*. The Cairngorms are the second richest site in Britain for montane vascular plants, with seventy-seven out of 118 possible species. They are the richest site in Britain for montane calcifuge plants, have a rich montane calcicole flora and a prolific snow bed and spring bryophyte flora.

12. *Landforms*. The Cairngorms have the most outstanding assemblage of erosion surfaces, tors, glacial and peri-glacial, meltwater and fluvial landforms in the country. The combination of features in a relatively small area is unique outside the Arctic.

Not all the above values were fully recognised when the National Nature Reserve was established. The first Reserve management plan identified the extent of high ground, the mountain flora and fauna, and the native pinewoods as the important features of the Cairngorms. The management objectives were to:

a. allow the area to evolve naturally, but subject to management based on observation, experience and experiment;

b. rehabilitate the disturbed areas, and notably the woodland felled in wartime;

c. carry out and facilitate research, especially research related to management;

d. maintain public access.

PAST MANAGEMENT FOR NATURE CONSERVATION

The history of NCC's management of the Cairngorms can be summarised under four headings:

Re-afforestation;   Publicity;

Red deer management;   Research and survey.

MAP 2: KEY

Enclosure	Location	Name	Area enclosed (hectares)	Year closed
1	Mar	Derry Wood	0.04	1956
2	Mar	Upper Glen Derry	0.05	1957*
3	Mar	Upper Glen Derry	0.07	1957*
4	Mar	Tom Dearg	2.5	1959
5	Invereshie	Creag Leathan	18	1959
6	Mar	Luibeg (1)	3.2	1960
7	Invereshie	Creag Ghiuthsachan	20	1964
8	Invereshie	Creag Mhigheachaidh	14.2	1967
9	Glen Feshie	Coille an Torr	130	1967
10	Glen Feshie	Ruigh-aiteachain (1)	0.6	1970
11	Invereshie	Allt a' Mharcaidh	16.2	1972
12	Glen Feshie	Achleum	0.6	pre 1973
13	Glen Feshie	Badan Mosach	33.6	1973
14	Glen Feshie	Ruigh-aiteachain (2)	5.0	1975
15	Glen Feshie	Ruigh-aiteachain (3)	1.0	1975
16	Glen Feshie	River Island	2.0	1975
17	Glen Feshie	Allt nam Bo	8.0	1975
18	Mar	Luibeg (2)	2.5	1981
19	Glen Feshie/ Invereshie	Badan Mosach/ Creag Leathan	130	1980
20	Mar	Glen Derry	1.7	1981
21	Mar	Carn Crom	1.5	1981
22	Mar	Luibeg Bridge (1)	–	1982
23	Mar	Luibeg Bridge (2)	–	1982
24	Mar	Luibeg Bridge (3)	–	1982
+25	Invereshie	Invereshie	603	1985

* Opened in 1977.
+ Invereshie ring fence enclosures 5, 7, 8 & 11.
Some planting was done in all enclosures except 12 and 20-24.

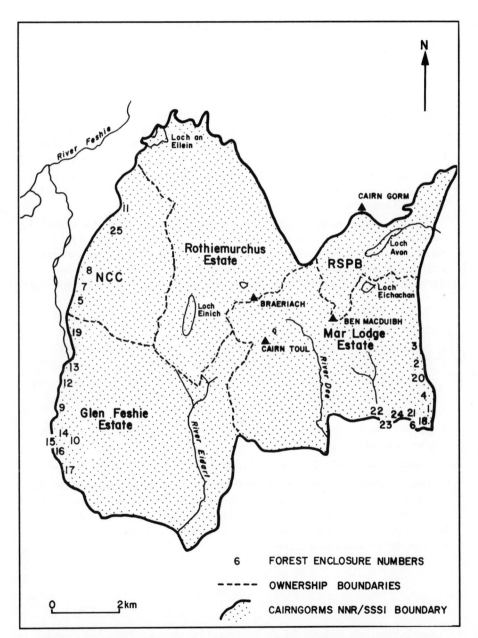

Map 2. Location of forestry enclosures used for regeneration experiments.

Re-afforestation (Map 2)

In the 1950s the Nature Conservancy's early work concentrated on the establishment of experimental plots in the Mar part of the Reserve where there were fewest signs of natural forest regeneration. Six hectares were enclosed and pine transplants from local sources were notch-planted and fertilised. In the 1960s, attention switched to land owned by the Nature Conservancy at Invereshie where sixty-eight hectares were enclosed and planted. In the first half of the 1970s, seventeen hectares were fenced in Glen Feshie. More native broadleaved trees were planted here, although Scots pine remained the main species. Meanwhile Glen Feshie estate planted 164 hectares on the NNR, using Scots pine and non-native conifers under a Forestry Dedication Scheme.

During these early years, it became apparent that the natural establishment of native trees and shrubs varied in the Cairngorms from patchy, but locally good, as in Rothiemurchus, to absent, as in Glen Feshie and Mar. Even in the worst areas, however, seedlings initially flourished in the vicinity of seed parent trees where they were protected from browsing pressure. Since 1975, NCC's management has concentrated on providing protection against browsing animals and encouraging the spread of the forest by natural regeneration.

1. A further six hectares were enclosed on Mar between 1980 and 1982.

2. In 1980, 130 hectares were enclosed at Badan Mosach near Achlean, jointly by NCC and Glen Feshie estate. Ten hectares in this enclosure have so far been planted by the estate using Glen Feshie provenance pine and the rest has been left to regenerate naturally.

3. In 1985 NCC completed a five kilometre ring fence on Invereshie enclosing 603 hectares.

4. Finally in 1987 NCC erected a forty hectare enclosure in Glen Derry.

Thus a total of approximately 820 hectares has been enclosed on the Reserve and effectively protected from browsing pressures and into which the native forest is now spreading. On the north-west side of the Reserve the balance between deer and trees is allowing substantial areas to regenerate without the protection of fences.

Red deer management

The Nature Conservancy acquired the stalking rights to Invereshie in 1954 and to Inshriach in 1966. Until 1964, eighteen stags and a few hinds were shot each year. Before 1975 the stag shooting was let as a sporting asset. The NCC took the shooting in hand in 1976 and since then has followed a policy directed at reducing the resident deer population. A major difficulty has been the presence of up to 400 wintering stags which could not be taken legally out of season. However their impact on natural regeneration has now been largely overcome by the ring fence at Invereshie.

Elsewhere on the Reserve the deer stalking is managed by the proprietors. There are very few deer on the high ground of Glen Avon on the RSPB's sector of the Reserve.

Because of their value for shooting and venison, deer form an important component of the economy of the private estates on the Reserve.

Publicity

The Conservancy's publicity efforts in the Cairngorms have varied. Several leaflets have been produced since the 1960s. The first major interpretive project was the Loch an Eilein nature trail, opened in 1966. This was followed by the opening of a nature trail at Achlean. In 1972 the Loch an Eilein visitor centre was opened in a restored cottage. Forty thousand people visited Loch an Eilein in the following year and ten thousand nature trail leaflets were sold. The Achlean trail was closed after six years to reduce disturbance to vulnerable nesting birds. For the six years between 1977 and 1982, NCC employed a Countryside Conservation Officer in the Aviemore Tourist Office. The Conservancy's mobile exhibition unit was based in the Coire Cas car park for two years and for one year NCC also leased a small office there for receiving visitors. In 1984 Rothiemurchus Estate terminated NCC's tenure of the Loch an Eilein visitor centre, and since then NCC has been without a focal point of contact with visitors to the Cairngorms NNR.

Research and survey

The Nature Conservancy Council controls research and survey on the Reserve and has been able to build up a data bank based on work done by its own staff, by contract or by third parties.

Current NCC staff research includes the mountain plateau project, which is investigating the impacts of damage and disturbance on the Cairn Gorm plateau. Recent surveys by NCC staff include a habitat survey and a vegetation survey of the Reserve, while current monitoring work includes an annual deer count, regular recording of the growth and regeneration of trees and shrubs, and measurement of browsing damage.

An example of recent contract work is the survey of the structure of the native forest in Rothiemurchus by Forest Conservation Services.

An example of one of the many monitoring and research projects undertaken on the Cairngorms by third parties is the Surface Waters Acidification Project which is being conducted by a consortium of Institutes on Invereshie.

In the late 1960s and early 1970s a major research programme was undertaken by the Range Ecology Research Group of the Nature Conservancy in Glen Feshie. A variety of research studies was completed here. The main programme was directed towards providing scientific advice to the estate in their programme to integrate forestry with deer management, but at the same time paying regard to the interests of nature conservation.

FUTURE MANAGEMENT : RATIONALE

The Nature Conservancy Council regularly reviews its policies for the management of National Nature Reserves. Council is revising the Cairngorms Management Plan at an appropriate time as two estates have recently changed hands and the Nature Reserve Agreements (NRA) with two others are being re-negotiated.

No other site in Britain matches the Cairngorms for the extent of its acidic montane and sub-montane vegetation, the continuous extent of ground above 800 metres, the range and variation of summit heath and snow bed communities, its unique arctic-alpine lochs and streams, and the low intensity of land use. The periglacial landforms, the faunal and floristic interest, the area's importance as a regional refuge for arctic-alpine species, and the native forest remnants of the Cairngorms are features which equal the best on other sites in Britain. The only other area in Britain comparable to the Cairngorms in ecological terms is the much less extensive and less varied granite massif of Lochnagar.

Above 800 metres in the Cairngorms, climax communities have persisted on fragile soils. Vegetation on the high ground recovers slowly from damage, and both soils and vegetation are vulnerable to the effects of trampling, muirburn and heavy grazing pressure.

Below 800 metres there has been considerable modification of the vegetation, which was probably once a complex of forest and scrub (see A. Watson this book), dominated by Scots pine and juniper and a restricted group of native broadleaved trees and shrubs. All but a tiny remnant of the sub-alpine scrub has vanished and much of the forest has been destroyed. The dwarf shrub heaths, grassland and bog communities which have replaced them have been maintained by management which has included grazing by domestic animals, muirburn and management of red deer herds at levels which usually limit or prevent tree and shrub regeneration. Despite these alterations, the vegetation communities on the lower ground have been less modified by man than most other areas in Britain below the tree line, except perhaps the blanket bogs on the flows of Caithness and Sutherland. Remoteness, low soil fertility and exposure are the reasons for this, and the evidence lies in the survival of a large number of extensive remnants of the native forest and a unique British example of an altitudinal treeline. Evidence from enclosures on and near the Reserve is that tree regeneration does take place at varying density in the absence of grazing by red deer and it is sufficient to replace the present stands in time. In unfenced parts of Rothiemurchus and Inshriach, natural regeneration has been sufficiently rapid and dense to restock the forest locally.

Red deer are an important component of the native fauna and are a sporting and meat-producing asset for the owners and an attraction to visitors. At present, high numbers of red deer prevent regeneration of trees and shrubs over much of the Cairngorms and there is some evidence of a reduction in the height of heather and a slow change from heather to grassland-dominated communities due to grazing pressure by red deer. Some soil erosion is also probably caused by heavy stocks of red deer in parts of the Cairngorms. A reduction in grazing pressure would encourage the recovery of other plant communities, notably tall herb vegetation. A heavy cull of red deer would need to be sustained over a number of years in some parts of the Cairngorms to reduce numbers appreciably, and deer from neighbouring estates may move in to replace them.

An alternative method to assist the forest to spread is to exclude deer by fencing the ground in rotation to protect the trees in their vulnerable early period of growth. However, this method produces blocks of even-aged pine with the appearance of plantations and without most of the native broadleaved species, which are usually barked by deer. Such a programme would be expensive in areas as high as the Cairngorms, where fences may often have to be replaced before tree leaders have grown above two metres and deer cannot be totally excluded from enclosures in times of heavy snow. On present scales of funding, such a programme would take more than a century to restore a forest ecosystem to the whole forest zone of the Reserve. Another alternative is to fence off large areas of lower ground or whole valleys, as at Glen Tanar and Invereshie, so as to provide extensive protection from browsing pressures for the development of the forest on a large scale.

Another main alternative is to fence and supplement natural regeneration by planting native species of local provenance. This would accelerate the process of restoring woodland and scrub, but involves a more intensive, more expensive and less natural a degree of management to speed up a process which would occur by less expensive methods but over a longer period of time.

The Cairngorms NNR has high scenic, recreational and wilderness values which with care can be mutually compatible with nature conservation. Wilderness–type recreation which does not require special facilities for its enjoyment conflicts with nature conservation in a few areas at certain times of the year, for example by disturbance to nesting birds and the destruction of vegetation and erosion of soil on the Cairn Gorm plateau. The building of the ski road and the chairlifts for downhill skiing has opened up the Cairn Gorm plateau to many more visitors. There has been a considerable spread of damage to vegetation and erosion of soil on this high ground since 1960 (Watson 1985).

Forestry and sport shooting are compatible in some respects with nature conservation, for example, the need to maintain and extend forest cover and the need to cull red deer and maintain stocks of game species. In other respects they are likely to conflict, and to do so acutely if the incentives for certain land uses increase. For example, commercial forestry would usually involve ploughing, fertilising, planting of exotic species and extraction of timber. Game management would involve the maintenance of red deer stocks at high levels, muirburn, predator control and the construction of access roads. Grazing by domestic animals would conflict with nature conservation through the need for muirburn, liming, fertilising and control of predators.

The main implications for management are that:

a. the near natural state of the Cairngorms communities is an important feature of the Reserve;

b. the high ground above the potential natural treeline has been damaged locally by public pressure; and

c. below the potential natural treeline, climax forest and scrub communities have been radically reduced or locally eliminated.

CONSTRAINTS ON MANAGEMENT

The main constraint on the Nature Conservancy Council's ability to pursue its own policies in the Cairngorms are the Nature Reserve Agreements. These Agreements give NCC limited rights on the NNR, for example, to appoint wardens, to carry out and control scientific research, and to erect notices and hides. The Agreements variously limit the owners' rights to carry out muirburn, to fertilise, to increase grazing pressures by domestic stock and to exploit peat and minerals, and impose restrictions on commercial forestry operations. Some of the Agreements also restrict the species which can be destroyed as game or pests, and ban the use of herbicides and pesticides. Under these Nature Reserve Agreements, NCC has no rights to control the public. NCC's ability to control forestry operations, the culling levels of red deer or the numbers of pest or game species which are destroyed is strictly limited. There is scope for the re-negotiation of terms which might provide NCC with greater control, and the Agreement with Rothiemurchus Estate is currently being re-negotiated.

It is apparent from discussions with the landowners of ground in the NNR that a reduction in the numbers of red deer to a level where tree and shrub regeneration would be successful without fencing throughout the Reserve is not acceptable to all of them. However, all proprietors support a programme for regenerating and extending the native forest and scrub. Some estates favour programmes involving rotational fencing to restock with Scots pine. Elsewhere, negotiations are proceeding on a revised Nature Reserve Agreement which will include a scheme involving strict protection of some areas of the native forest and controlled management elsewhere.

Some estates, pursuing game management policies, are not willing to abandon these entirely, even with compensation.

Other constraints on management for nature conservation include the statutory rights of other agencies, for example, the Forestry Commission's Dedication Agreements in Glen Feshie and the water authority's rights of access in Gleann Einich. The police have a right of access for law enforcement and supervision of mountain rescue operations. The public have well established rights of way on the Reserve.

FUTURE MANAGEMENT OPTIONS

Co-ordinated management is required to safeguard the quality of the large tracts of native forest, moorland and high plateau. NCC is the only management agency with an overall responsibility for conservation covering the Cairngorms National Nature Reserve. Policy should be directed to prevent fragmentation of the Reserve.

Compatible land use and the enforcement of strict planning policies to control development in the areas surrounding the Reserve and low-key management within the Reserve are required to perpetuate the near-natural qualities of the Reserve, to conserve the arctic qualities of the high ground and the communities of the summit-heaths, snow beds, arctic-alpine lochs and streams, lichen-rich heaths and blanket bog.

The Nature Conservancy Council has a responsibility to encourage the appreciation and study of the Reserve and to accommodate outdoor recreation activities, which depend on the natural qualities and character of the Reserve, provided these are compatible with the conservation of its natural features and do not require built facilities and mechanical aids.

Conservation of the communities of the high ground is best pursued by careful planning and management of access routes on to the Reserve so as to direct pressures on to the more robust and less ecologically important adjacent areas. This is considered to be more practicable than efforts to repair damage to summit areas, which would be expensive and would themselves constitute an intrusion into wilderness quality. Repairs should be limited to eroding footpaths and tracks on lower ground.

NCC has liaised closely with the planning authorities and with neighbours to try to ensure that developments adjacent to the Reserve are compatible with its conservation.

To this end it opposed the proposals for downhill skiing developments at Lurcher's Gully in 1981 and the snow fencing in Coire an t-Sneachda in 1986. NCC is opposed to any further skiing developments in the Northern Corries SSSI because of the direct impact such development would have on the SSSI and the indirect effect it would be likely to have on the National Nature Reserve.

Full recovery of the sub-alpine scrub and tall herb vegetation from the small fragments that survive today can be achieved only if muirburn and grazing pressures are reduced. The survival and spread of the forest requires the killing of deer. Ideally, deer numbers should be reduced to a level where the forest can spread and perpetuate itself without the need for fencing. In practice, and in the near future, this is likely to be achieved only in some parts of the Cairngorms. Elsewhere, fencing programmes will be undertaken to provide protection to young trees on a rotational basis.

The near-natural qualities of the Reserve will be enhanced if the Nature Reserve Agreements can be revised to phase out commercial forestry, to exclude domestic grazing animals and to eliminate game management other than deer stalking.

The emphasis for management by NCC of the Cairngorms NNR will be to give a positive lead in co-operation with others to establish strict protection of the rare natural and wilderness qualities of the Reserve by low-key management on the Reserve and the encouragement of sympathetic planning and land use on land adjoining the Reserve. In order to restore forest and scrub vegetation to the lower ground, more action will be required including steps to manage habitats, coupled where possible with control of red deer herds at levels which permit forest and scrub regeneration. The main emphasis on the protection of the fauna should be to influence public opinion by education, and by the careful siting and management of the main access points and routes on the NNR.

The operational objectives and outline prescriptions for the Cairngorms NNR are summarised in Table 1.

CONCLUSIONS

A number of steps need to be taken if the management of the Cairngorms is to meet the requirements of nature conservation. The deer cull has to be increased in parts of the Reserve and muirburn and grazing by domestic animals need to be prevented to provide appropriate conditions for the natural recolonisation of forest and scrub. Damage and erosion on the Cairn Gorm plateau must be reduced. This may be achieved by channelling visitors on to more robust ground or strengthened routes off the NNR, by providing alternative 'honeypots', and by providing the public with more information on the nature conservation values of the Cairngorms and with codes to guide their behaviour. The area surrounding the Cairngorms should be zoned to provide land uses and control of developments compatible with the maintenance and enhancement of the Reserve's interests. The key features of nature conservation should be monitored to ensure that appropriate action is taken in time to prevent any deterioration in values.

Finally, management for nature conservation should take account of the legitimate interests of informal outdoor recreation organisations, landscape and amenity bodies and the interests of the local community. Managers should seek common ground and identity of interests with the users of the Reserve. The key to the conservation of the Cairngorms in the future is the development of environmental awareness in the users of the Reserve, which fosters a recognition, acceptance and a cherishing of the international values of the Cairngorms.

REFERENCES

COUNTRYSIDE COMMISSION FOR SCOTLAND. (1978). *Scotland's Scenic Heritage.* Countryside Commission for Scotland, Perth.

HMSO. (1947). *National Parks and the Conservation of Nature (Scotland)*. Command Paper 7235, HMSO, London.

NATURE CONSERVANCY. (1959). *Cairngorms National Nature Reserve. Management Plan*. Nature Conservancy, Edinburgh.

NATURE CONSERVANCY. (1968). *Cairngorms National Nature Reserve Management Plan. First Revision*. Nature Conservancy, Edinburgh.

NATURE CONSERVANCY COUNCIL. (1985). *Cairngorms National Nature Reserve. Policy Guidelines*. Internal report, Nature Conservancy Council, Aberdeen.

NATURE CONSERVANCY COUNCIL. (1987). *Cairngorms National Nature Reserve. Interim Management Plan*. Nature Conservancy Council, Aberdeen.

RATCLIFFE, D.A. (1977). *A Nature Conservation Review*. Cambridge University Press, Cambridge (2 vols.).

SHIRT, D.B. ed. (1987). *British Red Data Book 2. Insects*. Nature Conservancy Council, London.

WATSON, A. (1985). Soil erosion and vegetation damage near ski lifts at Cairn Gorm. *Biological Conservation, 33*, 363-381.

POSTSCRIPT

The policies outlined here are those of the Nature Conservancy Council but the author is responsible if there are any errors in the way they are expressed.

TABLE 1

Operational Objectives and Outline Prescriptions

A. *Habitat Management*		*Outline Prescriptions*
1. Above 800 metres To allow the ecosystems to evolve with the minimum of interference.	Habitat Management *Option 1. Non intervention	1. Monitor damage to soils and vegetation, and disturbance to selected species. 2. Prevent grazing by domestic livestock. 3. Prevent muirburn.
2. Below 800 metres Restore native woodland and scrub and tall-herb communities	Option 3. Active Management	1. Prevent grazing by domestic stock. 2. Prevent muirburn and revise fire plan. 3. Protect Reserve with fire fighting equipment. Fight fires. 4. Construct fenced enclosures and ring fences in selected areas. 5. Survey enclosures at establishment. 6. Maintain fences in deer-proof condition. 7. Remove or kill red and roe deer, and control hares and rabbits within enclosures. 8. Monitor natural regeneration and damage to native trees and shrubs.
B. *Species management*		
1. To control red deer over parts of the Reserve at levels which will allow the restoration of native woodland and scrub by natural regeneration, and to monitor deer	Species Management Option 2. Control and reduction	1. Carry out annual count of red deer. 2. Carry out deer cull on NCC estate as necessary. 3. Liaise with estate owners in and around the Reserve over deer management, winter feeding, range improvement, etc.

management
policies over the rest
of the reserve

4. Eliminate deer, hares and
   rabbits within enclosures.

2. To allow other
   native species to
   evolve with a
   minimum of
   interference

Option 1
Non intervention

1. Renengotiate NRAs to
   eliminate sport shooting.
2. Monitor breeding success of
   selected species.
3. Kill foxes that are causing
   significant agriculture
   damage.
4. Protect Schedule 1 birds by
   wardening surveillance.

C. *Study and Research*

1. To carry out,
   contract and
   encourage study and
   research of direct
   application to the
   management of the
   Reserve and of
   benefit to nature
   conservation.
2. To permit other
   studies and research
   which cause no
   significant damage
   or disturbance and
   do not conflict with
   Objectives A and B.

Study & Research
Option 3.

Controlled facilities

1. Promote research, survey
   and monitoring projects
   that will aid management.
2. Prepare a summary of
   information and data
   requirements for the
   Reserve.
3. Encourage Universities and
   other appropriate
   organisations to carry out
   appropriate studies and
   research.
4. Control and monitor
   research use of the Reserve
   by maintaining the research
   permit system.
5. Collect information on the
   biological and physical
   features of the Reserve and
   on human impacts.

D. *Education and*
   Interpretation

To encourage the
appreciation and
study of the Reserve
for activities which

Option 3

Active Publicity

1. Provide information on the
   conservation and
   management of the Reserve
   and a code of conduct by

depend on its natural qualities and character and at levels which are compatible with its nature conservation, scenic and wilderness values.

Outline Prescriptions

Reserve signs, leaflets, talks and contacts with the media. Publish leaflets on: (a) Reserve management policies; (b) aspects of the natural history of the Cairngorms.

2. Establish a Visitor Centre on Speyside.
3. Review the provision of information at the main access points.
4. Develop a programme and code of conduct for use of the Reserve by schools.

E. *General Access and Recreation*

In recognition of its recreational values to encourage the use of the Reserve for activities which do not require built facilities or mechanical aids and provided such are compatible with its nature conservation scenic and wilderness values

Option 4
Open Access

No access permission required but some public uses are considered inappropriate

1. Monitor visitor use by appropriate surveys.
2. Monitor damage to vegetation and soils from footpath erosion.
3. Review management of mountain bothies.
4. Prepare plan for repair and maintenance of Lairig Ghru path.
5. Prepare plan for maintenance and repair of other paths.
6. Hold annual meeting with outdoor recreation organisations.
7. Liaise with HIDB and CCC with a view to reducing visitors impact on Cairn Gorm Plateau.
8. Prevent the development of built facilities.

F. *General management*
To minimise the
harmful effects of
development and
other activities on or
adjacent to the
Reserve on its
scientific, scenic or
wilderness values

1. Protect the Reserve by
   friendly but firm wardening
   service.
2. Protect the Reserve by
   regular liaison with owners
   and their staff. Hold regular
   meetings with owners.
3. Fulfil the legal obligations
   of the NRAs.
4. Protect the Reserve by
   regular liaison
   with its main users
5. Remove litter.
6. Protect the Reserve against
   harmful developments by
   liaison with the planning
   authorities.
7. Give advice to the planning
   authorities and neighbours
   on the effects on the
   Reserve of land use policies
   and developments near the
   Reserve.

G. *Reserve Records*
To maintain Reserve
records

1. Complete revision of the
   Reserve Management Plan
   1989-1994.
2. Revise policy guidelines.
3. Determine policies for the
   wider Cairngorm area.
4. Prepare Reserve
   monitoring plan.
5. Revise fire plan.
6. Carry out annual safety
   audit and check.
7. Log event records on a
   regular basis.
8. Maintain Project Register.

Outline Prescriptions

9. Prepare annual work schedule and financial estimates.
10. prepare annual progress report.
11. Submit monthly and special reports.
12. Inspect equipment and vehicles annually.
13. Maintain and replace equipment and vehicles.

*For further details of options see *Site Management Plans for Nature Conservation - a Working Guide* published by NCC.

MANAGING ROTHIEMURCHUS ESTATE

JOHN GRANT OF ROTHIEMURCHUS
Rothiemurchus Estate, Aviemore, Inverness-shire PH22 1QH

Rothiemurchus is the name of the land lying between the River Spey at Aviemore and the watershed of the Cairngorms. The varied landscape passes from low-lying fields and hardwoods around the rivers, through open moorland, mixed woodland, forestry plantations and the Old Caledonian pine forest. Beyond this rise the high hills with their own landscape of heather-clad foothills, lochs, boulder scree and high corries leading to the near arctic plateau which forms the summit of the Cairngorms. The high tops include Creag an Leth-choin, Braeriach and Sgoran Dubh lying above the Lairig Ghru and Gleann Einich. Rothiemurchus has been held by my family since the middle of the sixteenth century.

The total area of Rothiemurchus is 10 000 hectares and more than one million people come to see it every year. It is generally recognised as being an important part of the most important National Nature Reserve (NNR)in the United Kingdom – the Cairngorms National Nature Reserve (see Matthew; Curry-Lindahl this book). One of the main reasons for its importance is the large area of Old Caledonian pine forest, lying on an expanse of gravelly soils mostly unsuitable for arable farming. Stretching from the River Spey to Britain's highest natural tree line at about 600 metres, Rothiemurchus is superlative because of careful management of the forest over many centuries. The earliest record of a conservation policy being carried out on the Estate is in the papers of the Bishopric of Moray and dates back to the thirteenth century. It was then a condition of the granting of the lease of Rothiemuchus that the big pine trees for which the area was so well renowned, were not felled. The next written record of which I am aware was by William Grant in 1820, who pursued a policy of building dykes around the forests to prevent the farm animals grazing and preventing further natural regeneration. William Grant was also a great agricultural improver and carried out extensive draining schemes of the highly fertile lowlands adjacent to the River Spey. I am sure that William was not the first laird to care for the forest and certainly his policies were continued after his death. The Estate has suffered from severe struggles, poor economic conditions, unemployment and depopulation but never from the extremes of clearances of its people or trees. It has benefited from the continuing sale of timber peaking during the Napoleonic wars, the nineteenth century boom in field sports, the development of Aviemore as a railway junction, and, after the severe depression resulting from Dr Beeching railway cuts, from the development of Cairn Gorm as one of Scotland's foremost downhill skiing areas. For the past hundred years people have also enjoyed reasonable access to the hills for walking and climbing, and to a minor extent this has also brought employment.

The greatest threat to the conservation of the tops of the Cairngorms is their increasing popularity. The near-arctic plateau is easy land to walk on, and is very vulnerable to erosion, but control of people is neither desirable nor practical. Protection is possible only through control by education and persuasion. Our management at Rothiemurchus aims to expand visitor attractions in areas where the disturbance to nature by visitors is minimal, and to increase the public's awareness of our unique natural asset. We do not try to increase the numbers of people visiting the National Nature Reserve but it is our policy to create an awareness of its unique qualities and to ensure responsible use of it.

Until 1975, the policy at Rothiemurchus was to try to protect the Cairngorms by creating a 'honeypot area' at Loch an Eilein to which people were encouraged to go. The input from the Estate into the tourism industry was entirely passive and although many people appreciated the non-commercial attitude, it did not work. The worst problems arose from a lack of appreciation by the general public of the worth of the pinewood and the Cairngorms. This resulted in a benign neglect of these assets by the tourism industry, the local authority and the visiting public. Furthermore those people who did appreciate the natural interest were left unguided; they created more disturbance to wildlife and obtained little satisfaction. The result could only be described as a mess which manifested itself in inconsiderate wild camping, dogs out of control, litter, badly designed public works, a poor attitude to visitors by the local community and worst of all some severe forest fires in sensitive conservation areas.

In 1975, we changed the policy to one which is considerably more active and to a great extent follows modern commercial practice. We identify customer demand and aim to satisfy it. We create an awareness of the quality of experience that can be obtained so that visitors can sensibly decide on whether or not to visit Rothiemurchus. There is no point in attracting people who would be happier elsewhere.

A programme of communication was developed which increases appreciation and awareness through a colour leaflet and encourages responsible use through signs and a free footpath map and guide. This communication is not easy in Rothiemurchus as the conservation areas are intersected by over fifteen kilometres of busy public road. It is not possible to create a boundary and suggest that one side of it is more or less important than the other for any one particular interest. Different methods of communication must be used at different locations. A series of alternative 'honeypot' areas have been developed, many of which, such as the trout farm, are not in important conservation zones. These enable the conservation message to be given before 'nature' is disturbed. Indeed, many people are entirely satisfied by watching one of our many ospreys fishing at the fisheries loch and venture no further.

A Ranger Service, grant-aided by the Counryside Commission for Scotland, was set up in recognition of the freedom of public access provided by the Estate. We welcome and thank the Commission for this partnership. The Government carries its share for the public rights of access and privately we provide people with recreation facilities such as tours, fishing and shooting. Since 1981, legislation (the Wildlife and Countryside Act) has been provided for land holders to be similarly assisted with the financial burdens of national policies for nature conservation and as the Nature Conservancy Council (NCC) work through the list of Special Sites of Scientific Interest (SSSI), a similar partnership is developing on nature conservation matters.

The result is that the adopted national policies for the National Nature Reserve are entirely followed and legally binding. Also the estate is accepted as a responsible conservation organisation, as a significant part of the commercial tourist industry, and as a sensible, traditional land user. However, problems still remain and I will identify them as follows:

1. A general misunderstanding of the legislation relating to SSSIs makes it difficult for NCC to reach agreement with landholders. We should be asking ourselves why every landholder is not queueing up to have an SSSI. If the management agreements were seen to be satisfactory, NCC staff would find the notification of SSSIs more popular and therefore considerably easier to manage. There also appears to be a presumption by some people that management agreements are bad and should be fought at any stage. This attitude makes it difficult for NCC and landholders to reach satisfactory agreements. I feel the fault lies with officials who have not studied and properly understood land management, the Wildlife and Countryside Act, the financial guidelines and the requirements of modern conservation policies. Generally the Nature Conservancy Council now have a full understanding, especially where their staff are involved in negotiating agreements. These agreements do, however, have to be ratified by other officials who see them as allowing people to be paid for doing nothing. There are some people who would argue that the compensation payments are unnecessary but in my mind that is an argument to be aimed at the political level and should not affect current negotiations.

2. Nature conservation interests are often seen by local people to be extremist; it is not generally understood that the duty of the NCC is to advise

on conservation interests. It is not their position to compromise – in Scotland, this is left to the Secretary of State after taking due advice from his Departments. This position leaves NCC open to the criticism of not living in 'the real world'.

3. Some conservation groups and individuals are apt to make 'over the top' remarks which make it all too easy for other non-conservation groups to dismiss them and by implication others of like interests, as extremists and so weaken the conservation argument. Too often these remarks arise from people who have heard that an area has been proposed for development and claim that it has 'unique' interest and is a 'last surviving remnant', before other similar areas have been studied in equal detail.

4. Mountain bicycles are not suitable for the plateaux of the Cairngorms. They can cause erosion and, if used irresponsibly, tear up old pony paths. On the north side of the Cairngorms, we, in conjunction with the Forestry Commission, have developed a sensible policy for the use of mountain bicycles which appears to be accepted by all users. It would be most helpful if the Grampian side could come to some similar arrangement.

5. The Lairig Ghru footpath now attracts increasing numbers of walkers in general and also specifically more and more sponsored walks. These are now causing considerable damage to the peaty sections on the north side and we would like more guidance from hill walkers as to how they feel these sections should be maintained.

I am often asked how, with these problems in mind, I see the Cairngorms being managed in the future and I would like to outline my answers as follows:

On the north side of the Cairngorms there is a complex relationship between nature conservation, building conservation, historical interest, community interest, traditional land uses and tourism. I do not think that there is a valid argument for any one interest to exclude another and I believe that all can be sensibly integrated. Management will therefore best be continued by a partnership between private and public responsibility. To single out any area publicly as being particularly special would create additional commercial interest and pressures, and would also 'downgrade' the land outside. Possible problems are as follows:

   a. nature conservation interests can be adequately looked after by the Wildlife and Countryside (1981) Act once it is fully implemented. The problem is that implementation takes a lot of hard work and time, and so considerable patience is required;

   b. buildings and the historical infrastructure require much greater appreciation and interest and I would like to see traditional architectural features being continued to the exclusion of other styles. Finance and incentives have been provided for this in the English National Parks and I see no reason why a similar policy cannot be pursued within our National Scenic Areas in Scotland;

c. national scenic interests could be enhanced by declaring the glens and straths around the Cairngorms as Environmentally Sensitive Areas (ESA), thereby maintaining the traditional pattern of open field and old forest. It must be remembered that the agricultural land is also an important habitat for our wildlife and contributes greatly to our scenery.

I do not think it is desirable or necessary to set up some new bureaucracy to achieve the practical aims of caring for the high mountains. The challenge for people in conservation today is to persuade the majority of people in this country that it is worthwhile to spend their money on those matters which we care about, and to present it so that those people who live on the land perceive conservation as being in their interest. Much good work has been done in comparing our achievements with those of overseas countries but much of this work has been undone by thinking that national or international conservation interests should override the views and wishes of local communities.

CHAIRMAN'S REMARKS FOR SECOND SESSION
THE WILL TO SUCCEED

J.W.H. CONROY

Institute of Terrestrial Ecology, Banchory AB3 4BY

In the earlier papers we read of the problems involved in managing parts of the Cairngorms – the cases for development, conservation, and how the local resident landowner sees his role and problems.

Two points are clear:

1.   Many people still disagree on the effects that developments might have on the Cairngorms, or the scientific value of parts of the area such as the Northern Corries SSSI, and on the level of conservation necessary.

2.   There is a need for sound, impartial, scientific research, as a basis upon which sensible decisions can be made.

What is required first and foremost is the will from all groups to examine critically the appropriate available information and from there strive for the best protection of this unique environment.

PRESSURES ON THE FORESTS OF THE CAIRNGORMS

B.M.S. DUNLOP

*Forest Conservation Services, Lynemacgregor, Grantown-on-Spey,
Morayshire PH26 3PR*

SUMMARY

Because of climatic deterioration and man's exploitation, the natural pine and birch forests of the Cairngorms have been in decline for some 4000 years. In recent times the main pressures have been from felling, planting, browsing and burning, but since 1981 the Wildlife and Countryside Act has achieved greater protection. Provided that this is increased, that threats from pollution are closely monitored, their levels reduced, and catastrophies avoided, there is every reason to believe that the forests of the Cairngorms will survive and expand.

INTRODUCTION

The forests of the Cairngorms are defined as the natural woodlands on the slopes of the Cairngorms. These exclude plantations and the birchwoods of the lower straths, which have their own problems and pressures.

The forests of Scots pine and birch in the Cairngorms are remnants of the Old Caledonian forest which once covered most of northern Scotland. They have survived because they occupy sites which were and are generally too isolated, inhospitable or impoverished for economic agriculture or forestry. Some also owe their survival to the policies of enlightened owners.

The forests are best represented on the northern slopes of the Cairngorms, ranging from Abernethy through the Pass of Ryvoan to Glen More and Rothiemurchus, and then on to Invereshie and Glen Feshie in the west. On the southern side of the Cairngorms there are important remnants at Glen Derry, Glen Luibeg, Glen Lui, and Glen Quoich on Mar, while a few scattered mature pine are found at other locations such as Glen Avon in the east. The large pine forests at Ballochbuie and Glen Tanar in Deeside are not discussed below, as they do not lie on the lower slopes of the main Cairngorms massif.

The larger pinewoods such as those at Abernethy and Rothiemurchus are especially valuable because they contain a wide range of tree and shrub species, which in turn have ensured the survival of a wide variety of distinctive plant and animal species.

CLIMATE

Major changes in climate from about 4000 years ago led to increased wind and precipitation, and lower summer temperatures. The forests contracted as conditions for tree growth deteriorated. The natural treeline gradually dropped from around 800 metres to about 500 metres, and there was a spread of blanket peat and bogs. These conditions still exist and inhibit tree growth in the Cairngorms. Depending on topography, they limit the timberline to about 500 metres.

PRESSURES ON THE FORESTS
Commercial forestry

Early exploitation of the trees was probably confined to the establishment of small clearings by axe and fire for the growing of farm crops and the grazing of domestic stock. Small amounts of timber would also have been cut for local needs such as building materials, furniture, tools and implements, fencing and fuel.

From 1600 onward, large-scale fellings for shipbuilding on the Moray coast and export to the south severely depleted the more accessible parts of the Strathspey forests, and from around 1750 restocking was mainly by planting. Such commercial forestry continued into the 1980s and, until recently, these fellings and plantings were a serious threat to the survival of the few remnants of naturally regenerated forest.

The Wildlife and Countryside Act of 1981 has considerably relieved this pressure in most areas. Owners are now able to enter into agreement with the Nature Conservancy Council whereby their forestry operations are restricted in the most sensitive areas, but they do not suffer financial loss as a result. Most of the natural forests in the Cairngorms are now in areas designated as National Nature Reserves (NNR) or Sites of Special Scientific Interest (SSSI), and most lie within the Cairngorms National Scenic Area.

However there is still some pressure, mainly from planting schemes involving public funding by direct planting grant and Schedule D tax concessions. Despite being inappropriate in natural woodlands, these have led to further loss of native pinewood, for example in Abernethy in the mid 1980s.

It was announced in the budget of March 1988 that the Schedule D concession was to be withdrawn, with a transitional period of tax reliefs until 1993. A review of the Native Pinewoods Grant Scheme, which at present allows the planting of bare sites within existing pinewood boundaries, is due early in 1989.

Browsing

The general lack of natural regeneration throughout the Cairngorms is causing widespread concern. Although a hostile climate and ground conditions restrict tree establishment on many sites, there is overwhelming evidence that browsing pressure from red deer is the main cause of tree loss between the seedling and sapling stages. Throughout the upper forest, deer densities are too high to permit tree establishment in all areas except those where regeneration is so plentiful that it can withstand browsing simply by force of numbers. The abnormally low representation of broad-leaved species is almost entirely due to browsing. Where there is a reduction of pressure through protection (for example, rock faces or fencing) and disturbance (near roads or paths), regeneration is able to proceed. In some of the lower forest, where red deer are rare or excluded, appreciable areas of successful regeneration are common in Abernethy, Ryvoan, Glen More and Rothiemurchus.

Burning

The natural forest is a 'moving' forest – regeneration tends to be more successful in the lee of mature stands, due to the higher seedfall. Pine and birch are pioneer species, which colonise adjacent bare sites more readily than partially stocked areas, as they grow best in full light as opposed to partial shade.

Outwith the present forest boundaries, the main land use is often grouse moor, which is subject to periodic muirburn. Young trees regenerating on such sites are burnt, while more mature trees which survive the flames are sometimes felled. Muirburn not only prevents expansion which in turn would increase the overall forest area, but may also reduce replacement opportunities for some mature stands. Unable to restock within the stand due to shade, or outwith due to burning, regeneration may be prevented during the period of optimum seed production.

Muirburn is therefore a threat to natural woodland expansion, and buffer zones between forest and grouse moor should be retained for extension. However, it must be acknowledged, that regular burning creates good conditions for regeneration, mainly by reducing the thick moss layer which prevents seed from reaching the ground. Where grouse moors are abandoned or frequent burning is discontinued, tree cover may quickly become established. This can now be observed in various parts of Deeside, Strathdon and Strathspey.

Other Threats

Although not pressures, other agencies can threaten forest survival locally.

These include:

1. *Fire.* Public access inevitably increases the risk of fire, while at the same time increases the chance of early detection. In practice, most fires originate on forest margins, for example on roadsides or from careless muirburn, and are generally readily accessible for fire-fighting.

2. *Disease.* Fungal or insect attacks can cause serious damage, but the ancient forests normally have in-built natural controls which considerably reduce the risk of widespread loss.

3. *Storms.* Severe gales and hurricanes may cause a loss of mature trees from windthrow. Such damage tends to be localised, however, and is part of the natural cycle, so the forests normally recover.

4. *Pollution.* At present there is little evidence of major problems from air pollution in the Cairngorms, but some potentially serious effects have been observed elsewhere and we should be aware of these implications.

For example, recent research (Scottish Development Department 1988) suggests that acid deposition exacerbates natural soil acidification over a relatively short period of time, especially on afforested deep peat in mountain areas with high precipitation. Hill peats have acidified to an extent that is restricting the growth of acid-tolerant species and encouraging the spread of nitrate-tolerant species, resulting in a decline of vegetation such as heather and an expansion of species such as purple moor grass which may be less amenable to pine regeneration.

On a global scale, the 'greenhouse' effect is causing climatic change, and any such alteration to the environment is potentially damaging. Cold, wet weather in spring and summer has been recorded locally in the last few years, and such conditions can reduce the length of the growing season and reduce flower, pollen and therefore seed production and dispersal, which in turn reduces regeneration. Mild winters can result in premature bud opening, and can increase fungal and insect survival.

The thinning of the ozone layer increases radiation which is harmful to plant life, including trees. It is therefore of vital importance that all forms of air pollution are minimised, and their effects on the environment closely monitored.

REFERENCES

SCOTTISH DEVELOPMENT DEPARTMENT (1988). *Symposium on Acidification in Scotland 1988.* Scottish Development Department, Edinburgh. (Abstracts only).

HUMAN IMPACT ON THE CAIRNGORMS ENVIRONMENT ABOVE TIMBER LINE

ADAM WATSON

Institute of Terrestrial Ecology, Banchory AB3 4BY

SUMMARY

1. The main human impact on what is now open hill ground in the Cairngorms was large-scale deforestation centuries ago. Boreal forest and subalpine scrub were turned into moorland, which has been kept open since then by sheep and deer browsing and by burning. Important impacts in past centuries were the settlement of human populations on farms in the glens, and subsequent dereliction due to landowners' clearances and depopulation by voluntary emigration of tenant farmers. Other large past impacts were the lodges, bothies, tracks and footpaths built for game shooting, and many tree plantations set up on moorland.

2. Since 1940, human impacts have increased rapidly. The numbers of hill walkers and other visitors have risen greatly, especially where access has been made easier by new roads or chairlifts, and where such attractions have been strongly promoted.

3. Ski developments have caused much vegetation damage and soil erosion. Easier access from the Cairn Gorm ski ground has spread these impacts on to the Cairn Gorm – Ben Macdui plateau, the most outstanding area in Britain for arctic-like features.

4. Since 1960, many hill tracks have been bulldozed to make access easier for the shooting of deer and grouse, including ground on the Cairngorms National Nature Reserve. These tracks caused scars on the landscape and greatly reduced the size of roadless areas.

5. On the deer forests, poorly controlled or uncontrolled muirburn has usually covered large areas at a time, occasionally more than a square kilometre, and has often been too hot, leading to burning of the soil.

6. Over much of the area, high stocks of red deer have increased greatly. These have prevented tree extension on to the moorland from most of the relict patches of Old Caledonian forest and birch. In many places, moorland next to Old Caledonian woods has been fenced, ploughed and densely planted with conifers, including exotic species, on as well as off the Cairngorms National Nature Reserve. On land that is not heavily populated by red deer, a rundown of arable farming in the glens and a lessening of muirburn have been followed by large-scale colonisation of moorland by naturally regenerating pines and birches. However, increasing amounts of

this have been lost in recent years by intensive afforestation.

7. Conservation designations have failed to prevent a big decline in the area's wild qualities. Many organisations with different aims have responsibility for the area, but no one organisation has predominance; the result has been increasing and continual conflict. Public funding has supported developments that reduced the area's wild qualities, such as new ski roads and tows, and intensive afforestation.

INTRODUCTION

The aim of this paper is to provide a factual, impartial review of human impact on what is now open hill ground in the Cairngorms. Human-induced changes have been occurring there for centuries, and the paper opens with a brief historical account of these past influences. However, numerous major impacts have taken place this century, especially in the last thirty years, and the area is now affected by increasing and unprecedented human pressures and developments. At the same time, concern about the area has grown rapidly, and groups with different interests have come increasingly into conflict. Objective scientific research by non-campaigning bodies is important for identifying such problems in an unbiased manner and providing a reliable basis for other bodies to take rational decisions on alternative solutions. This paper is based mainly on detailed research on human impact between 1967 and 1988. In addition, I have made observations and notes on human impact there since 1943, and have interviewed many old residents in order to get information back to the 1890s. As this paper is a factual review, it does not give or imply value judgements as to whether a given change is good or bad.

'Human impact' involves obvious changes such as bulldozed tracks, ski developments and tree plantations. It also has more subtle effects on the qualities of wilderness and other wild land in the Cairngorms; 'wilderness' and 'wilderness qualities' are as defined by Watson (1984a, 1988a). Those who wish to maintain wilderness qualities in the world regard the perception of natural beauty, solitude, absence of human artifacts, and risks to human life and limb, as positive benefits. Most of the human impact on the area has involved a decline in wild qualities.

By the 'Cairngorms' I mean not just the main massif of Am Monadh Ruadh between Rothiemurchus on Speyside and Braemar on Deeside, but also the surrounding land including that part of the hill range of Am Monadh (The Mounth) from Drumochter to near Ballater. This is approximately the 4000 square kilometres of the 1967 Cairngorm Area report, as described by Balharry (this book).

'Timber line' means the actual present upper limit of commercial timber, not the potential upper limit over the large tracts where the land is open and treeless because of deer and sheep browsing and burning.

HISTORICAL ACCOUNT UP TO 1940

By far the biggest human impact was the deforestation of most ground below 600 metres and its replacement by moorland dominated by heather. It appears that deforestation in the east Highlands was largely due to man's activities (Birks 1970; O'Sullivan 1976) involving forest clearance for settlement but probably also for grazing by domestic stock. Much of this destruction of the boreal forest had taken place by about the eleventh century, and forest clearance had almost finished by the time that the early map-makers and estate surveyors recorded the extent of woodland in the 1600s and 1700s. Blaeu's *Atlas Novus* in 1654 shows woodland of similar extent to the area of natural woodland this century, so 'probably the main forest cover had already disappeared by 1654' (Nethersole-Thompson & Watson 1981). The Speyside forests that were exploited in the 1700s and 1800s are still there, because felling was followed by regeneration and woodland management. Gloomy statements (Ritchie 1920; Darling 1947; Darling & Boyd 1969) 'about deforestation due to commercial exploitation of the timber, using examples from Speyside, are therefore misleading' (Nethersole-Thompson & Watson 1981).

The second biggest human impact was the removal of virtually all subalpine scrub in a zone between 600 metres and the lower limit of the arctic-alpine ground at about 800 metres, and its transformation into open moorland dominated by heather. In other northern countries where man-induced burning and browsing are less intense, an extensive zone of subalpine scrub stretches above timber line, but in the Cairngorms it appears only in small patches, especially on cliff ledges free from fire and browsing animals. Fencing also leads to its spread. The habitat type that has suffered the biggest reduction in the Cairngorms is subalpine scrub (Watson 1977). Like woodland, nearly all of it had already gone by the late 1700s and early 1800s when the detailed descriptions of hill ground by the first estate surveyors show broadly the same picture as today. It is not known what caused the disappearance of subalpine scrub, but probably it was browsing and burning. Until the 1800s, many local people summered at shielings on the higher glens and hill pastures, and it is known that cattle and sheep numbers were high. Also, the Earl of Fife wrote in 1786 of 'the glens much burnt and may be preserved better' (Watson 1983).

The third biggest human impact in terms of area was the settlement of small populations on partly-arable farms in the lower glens. Later, a few of these populations were evicted by landowners' clearances for sheep and deer (Nethersole-Thompson & Watson 1981). Most of the populations that had not been evicted disappeared later by the voluntary emigration of tenant farmers. This spread over a longer period lasting up to the present decade. Some of the former farmlands were enclosed for sheep or cattle, but most of them provided fertile, sheltered grasslands for red deer.

Most of the formerly inhabited glens are now completely empty of people, and the rest are either virtually empty or severely depopulated. The hundreds of ruined farms that still remain are the most obvious reminder today. This contrasts strikingly with the thriving communities in mountainous parts of Switzerland and Norway (Watson & Watson 1983a, 1986) and in some other parts of Scotland (Rennie 1986; Callander 1987). In these cases, owner-occuiership of farms and other resources is associated with lower rural depopulation. The extinction of many human communities in the Cairngorms has made these glens more wild than when they were populated. However, this is man-induced dereliction, not wilderness. The air of dereliction is most obvious where the farms became vacant this century, as many of the buildings are still largely intact, although with broken roofs, windows and floors.

When the best soils in many glens changed in use from arable fields into feeding pastures for red deer, this doubtless helped increase deer numbers greatly (Nethersole-Thompson & Watson 1981). In addition, severe actions by landowners against poaching (Watson & Allan 1986) led to rapid increases in deer numbers in the late 1700s (Watson 1983).

The boom in deer and grouse shooting from the mid 1800s onwards caused further changes, particularly the building of new private roads, shooting lodges, houses and bothies in the upper and lower glens, and the building of many new footpaths on to the hills. A secondary consequence was the extermination of the pine marten, polecat and red kite, and severe reductions in the numbers and range of several other predators such as the wild cat. In the period 1920-40 the employment of deer stalkers, gamekeepers and others on sporting estates declined greatly, and many lodges, houses and bothies were deserted; most have since become ruins. This process has continued.

An important change since the late 1700s was the formation of large tree plantations on moorland. These plantations were mainly of Scots pine, with some larch and Norway spruce. As the trees were planted at a lower density than today, some of these early plantations of Scots pine now look quite like Old Caledonian woods, and have much blaeberry and other plants under the trees. Even the plantations established on moorland in the 1920s and early 1930s were of this open type.

HUMAN IMPACT SINCE 1940

General increase of hill visitors

Walkers, mountaineers and others visiting the Cairngorms and other Scottish hills have increased greatly in numbers since the second world war (Nethersole-Thompson & Watson 1981; Aitken 1985). Counts of people on the hills have shown about ten times as many on the Derry side of the Cairngorms massif since 1962 as in the 1940s, and respectively over twenty times as many on the Spey side of the Lairig Ghru path (Watson 1981, 1984b). These larger numbers led to an increase in the number and length of new footpaths, especially in places near roads which were open to the public and which gave easy access to attractive high hills such as Lochnagar. Heavy use of footpaths and the lack of annual maintenance on most of them in turn led to most paths becoming wider, rougher and wetter (Bayfield 1973; Aitken 1985).

Other problems that have followed the large increase of visitors are more litter, more hot fires in summer on moorland and in woodland, and deliberate severe damage to bothies, lodges and other buildings.

New bridges, huts and signs

When the Nature Conservancy erected new footbridges with the help of the Cairngorm Club at Corrour, Derry Dam and Glas Allt Mor in the early 1950s, hill walkers generally welcomed them. However the occasional damage to the Nature Conservancy's signs on the National Nature Reserve was a portent of a change in attitudes. Many hill walkers now dislike bridges, signs, hilltop indicators and new huts in the wilder parts of Scotland. New huts were allowed to be built in the middle of the Cairngorms National Nature Reserve in the 1960s. The Curran Hut at Lochan Buidhe on the Ben Macdui plateau went up without planning permission in 1967. Although this intruded on the wilderness quality of this area and also posed big risks to mountain safety, very few objected to it. Curran Hut proved important in the Feith Buidhe disaster in November 1971, when a party of Edinburgh schoolchildren died in a snowstorm while trying to reach the hut (Watson & Duff 1972). After much controversy it was demolished in 1975. Jean's Hut in Coire an Lochain was a somewhat similar case, and was demolished in 1986. Four metal huts or refuges still stand. When the bridge over Glas Allt Mor in Glen Derry became dangerous after a flood in the late 1970s, the change in attitudes showed clearly in the action by the Nature Conservancy

Council (NCC) to remove the bridge and not replace it, and in the lack of demands by hill walkers for a replacement. A proposal by the Scottish Rights of Way Society to erect a footbridge at Ath nam Fiann over the River Avon in 1987 led to much opposition, and subsequently to Moray District Council refusing planning permission.

Thousands of cairns have proliferated along paths and elsewhere, particularly in heavily used parts of the Cairngorms. Many hill walkers dislike these cairns and demolish them, but the activities of the cairn builders have generally outweighed those of the demolishers. Cairns on the remote high plateaux are an intrusion on wilderness qualities and pose risks to mountain safety by tempting inexperienced walkers to stray there.

Memorials on wild land raised no serious objections before the 1970s but increasingly cause controversy now. When plaques commemorating the centenary of Rotherham Council were erected on four summits in the Cairngorms in 1971, they were swiftly and anonymously removed.

Outdoor centres in Glen More

An army hut was built in 1950 on Castle Hill in Rothiemurchus and has since been extended to become the 'Union Jack Hut', which is a large building. A new road was made from Loch Morlich to the hut. These developments were far from existing settlements, gave much easier access to the Lairig Ghru, Braeriach and other hills, and led to heavier use of the Cairngorms by large, organised parties.

Other new outdoor centres have been built far from villages, notably the Scottish Sports Council's Glenmore Lodge and the Norwegian House at Glen More. These too have led to increased human pressures on hill ground near Glen More, particularly on Cairn Gorm and its plateau.

Boundaries for the Cairngorms National Nature Reserve

Nethersole-Thompson (1952) pointed out that the most outstanding high ground in the Cairngorms for birds was the Cairn Gorm – Ben Macdui plateau. It is also the foremost part for various arctic-like features (Watson 1981). When the Cairngorms National Nature Reserve was declared in 1954, the northern parts of the plateau inside the Glen More National Forest Park were not included. One result was that the northern slopes of Cairn Gorm and its corries were given less protection than the northern slopes of Braeriach, although the Braeriach slopes and plateau were less outstanding for birds and arctic-like features than the Cairn Gorm – Ben Macdui plateau. Some early exploration for skiing development involved Braeriach, which had good natural snow-holding, but then turned to Cairn Gorm. Cairn

Gorm was less strictly protected and was not owned by private landowners, so proposals there were less likely to run into objections from the Nature Conservancy and private landowners. The fact that the Northern Corries were not a Site of Special Scientific Interest (SSSI), let alone part of the National Nature Reserve, helped pave the way for proposals for large ski developments in the Northern Corries, which subsequently led to the Lurcher's Gully Public Inquiry in 1981. After the Inquiry, the NCC designated the Northern Corries as an SSSI.

Cairn Gorm roads and ski developments

The new road to Cairn Gorm in 1960 caused a large decrease in the area of wild, roadless terrain in the Cairngorms. Part of the road above the Glen More wood had steep, sharp corners, and was abandoned; it has not been properly reinstated. A second road also proved inadequate, so the third, 'Link' road was made by the army in 1981, and is now used along with the second road. Stewart (1986) showed that a fourth route would have necessitated only one road and would have been less prone to closure. He also pointed out that the construction of the three roads caused much scarring of hillsides and marred the view from Loch Morlich and Strath Spey generally. The Cairn Gorm road has always been open to cars at all seasons. In areas of high quality for scenery abroad, a frequent option for protecting the environment has been to ban private cars and use a smaller road for buses only, with a small bus park at the end, or to use other forms of transport that do not require a road.

In the early years of the skiing developments at Cairn Gorm, the operators used tracked vehicles on the open hillside for construction work and maintenance, bulldozed some pistes, and removed numerous boulders. This caused much vegetation damage and soil erosion (Watson 1967; Bayfield 1971, 1974), which reached a peak in 1968 at Coire Cas. Since then the amount of damage has been lower, as the operators channelled vehicles and walkers on to gravel roads, flew in new pylons, concrete and snow fencing by helicopter, and reduced erosion by reseeding bare ground with grass. Changes in ground management in 1987, for example at 'The Hump' in lower Coire Cas, were made so carefully that only experienced observers would have noticed them afterwards.

The all-season running of the chairlifts brought the summit of Cairn Gorm within easy reach of summer tourists. During surveys in 1971, 1973 and 1981, 700-900 people per day were counted walking from the top of the chairlift to the summit of Cairn Gorm during fine weather in July and August (Morris, Hammond & Kessler 1974; Gilmore 1975; Anderson Semens Houston 1981). This human impact damaged much vegetation and led to soil erosion on the upper parts of Cairn Gorm outside the ski pistes (Watson 1985), reaching a peak in 1981 (Watson in press).

Wherever large areas of bare ground are exposed, run-off after rain is faster and floods are more likely. On the Allt Mor, the main stream below Coire Cas, the frequency of severe flash floods increased greatly after the ski developments (Watson 1981), rising to an average rate of one flood per two years in 1970-81. Floods severely damaged the road, bridge and trees. Since 1981, the condition of the ground on the upper parts of Cairn Gorm has improved (see below and Watson in press). As expected from this, flash floods have become less frequent.

The easy access provided by the road to Coire Cas and the all-seasons running of the chairlift to the upper part of Cairn Gorm attracted many people on to the plateau south of Cairn Gorm and to a lesser extent into the Northern Corries (Watson 1967). Since the Coire Cas road and chairlifts opened in 1960-61, visitor numbers in July on the plateau have been approximately a hundred-fold what they were in 1943-59 (Watson 1981, 1984b). Minimum counts of visitors on the plateau in May-October increased from year to year to reach a peak mean of sixty nine per day in 1974 (Watson 1981). Since then, annual minimum counts have fluctuated at a slightly lower mean annual level of 34-63 per day, although much higher than the 3-37 in the 1960s.

As on Cairn Gorm, this big increase of people led to more bare ground and soil erosion on the plateau (Watson 1985), especially on exposed parts where most of the ground was already naturally bare because of the severe climate and poor soils. Lichens near footpaths on the plateau showed more damage than further away (Bayfield, Urquhart & Cooper 1981), and Watson (1985) found that lichens, heaths and herbs were scarcer on ground that was heavily disturbed by people than on nearby, seldom visited ground. The large increase of people also led to new footpaths developing over the plateau and into the Northern Corries, and beyond (Watson 1984b). The main concentration of new footpaths in the Cairngorms now radiates outwards from the car park and chairlifts at Coire Cas. The numerous visitors also gave rise to other human impacts on the plateau, such as the building of hundreds of cairns, and the killing of grass by stones removed by campers to weigh down their tents. Litter increased, especially at summits, and at snow patches where large organised parties practised snow-holing on winter survival courses.

Features of disturbed ground on the plateau generally declined in frequency between 1981 and 1988, including less soil erosion (Watson 1989). I have attributed this partly to fewer people visiting the plateau in summer and partly to a run of good growing seasons for plants and long snowy winters. However this improvement would be expected to reverse if summer visitors were to increase to their mid 1970s levels.

Another consequence of heavy human pressures on Cairn Gorm was that food scraps dropped by people attracted crows to the arctic-alpine ground (Watson 1979). They robbed many nests of ptarmigan, to the extent that the breeding success of ptarmigan on Cairn Gorm has been much lower since the ski developments than it was before, or than it has been on other hills nearby where crows have been absent (Watson 1981, 1982).

Ptarmigan and red grouse are at risk from flying into overhead cables at ski developments, and many have died from this cause. Breeding numbers of ptarmigan were previously high on Cairn Gorm, but on the most heavily developed part of Coire Cas have been virtually zero during summer in the 1980s, due largely to collisions with wires in spring (Watson 1981, 1982, in press). Other changes following the ski developments were that sheep, semi-domestic reindeer and mountain hares were attracted to the reseeded grassy patches (Watson 1979). In the early years, some people became concerned that the number of dotterel on the Cairn Gorm plateau would be reduced by human disturbance or by habitat damage due to trampling, but a study of dotterel numbers shows no such effect so far, either at Cairn Gorm or in the Mounth south of Braemar (Watson 1988b). Similarly, the numbers of snow buntings summering on the Cairn Gorm plateau have not been lower since the developments (Milsom & Watson 1984).

Other skiing developments

As at Cairn Gorm, the operators at the 'Glenshee' ski centre south of Braemar also used tracked vehicles on the open hillside for construction work and maintenance in the early years, and these caused much bare ground (Watson 1967, 1988c). However, soils there are deeper and more fertile than over the granite at Cairn Gorm, and vegetation recovered more quickly. The result was that little soil erosion occurred. Recent ski tows there have penetrated into an SSSI and into the Caenlochan National Nature Reserve, and the local authorities and the ski company have agreed on the need for technical environmental advice and monitoring, which are being provided by the Institute of Terrestrial Ecology (Glenshee Chairlift Company 1987). As a result, ground management for the Glas Maol Tow in 1986 was of the highest standard at any Scottish ski centre until that time.

The Lecht Ski Centre started in 1978. The company removed construction debris more carefully than the Cairngorm and Glenshee companies had done in their early years. However, tracked vehicles and skiers caused much bare ground within a few years. The Lecht slopes were mainly over deep peat, which provides poor conditions for reseeding and for the reestablishment of indigenous hill plants. The Company sought advice about the bare ground (Watson & Watson 1983b). In 1984 the District Councils made environmental advice and monitoring a condition of planning permission for new developments (Lecht Ski Company 1986). This was the first time that this type of cooperative management had occurred at a Scottish ski centre, but the precedent has now been followed at Glenshee Ski Centre also. At the Lecht it led to more expertise and sharing of knowledge, less damage to the hill, more successful reinstatement, optimum lines for pistes, towlines and snow fences, improved treatment of car-park verges and roadside verges, and less conflict with other interests. As a result, the increasing damage at the Lecht was stemmed, and since 1984 the amount of bare ground has fluctuated but with no obvious trend for the worse. Indeed, heath rush and cotton grass started to colonise wet bare peat on heavily trampled places in 1987, and this should lead to a tougher native vegetation replacing the reseeded swards.

Scottish ski centres depend on snow concentrated by drifting, and early developments at Cairn Gorm and the Glenshee area relied on naturally good snow-holding areas in sheltered hollows where snow tended to pile up during storms. Since then, snow-holding has been created and extended using snow fencing and piste machines.

A feature at all Scottish ski centres, which is particularly obvious at the Lecht, is that the extra snow-lie from snow fencing leads to a change in vegetation, even if vehicles and skiers cause no vegetation damage. The extra snow-lie encourages snow moulds to grow on heather more than usual, and this kills much of it. Heather is also more susceptible to bruising than most other plants on the slopes. As a result, heather has been largely replaced by grasses and blaeberry on snow-fenced towlines and pistes at the Lecht, and the same effect can be seen to a lesser extent at Cairn Gorm and Glenshee. The new sward is more resilient to further damage from piste machines and skiers than the heather sward was, and provides a smoother surface for skiing. Even a light snowfall can provide skiing on such short vegetation, whereas on the rank heather that was previously there it took a heavy snowfall to give any skiing. These new swards are still changing. Even in places where there is no vegetation damage or soil erosion, such as alongside but outside a snow fence, the vegetation will change. This was not realised by NCC or other bodies in earlier years, but was pointed out at the Lurcher's Gully Public Inquiry as a result of measurements on Cairn Gorm (Watson 1981). It has since been amply confirmed by measurements at the Lecht and Glenshee ski centres (e.g. Watson & Leitch 1987; Glenshee Chairlift Company 1987).

Other impacts at all three ski developments

At all three ski centres, gulls have increased in summer at the car parks and nearby, where they scavenge for waste food. Flocks of snow buntings in winter have also been more frequent at car parks, buildings, and nearby slopes than on remote hill ground of comparable area.

The main impact at all ski centres has been the visual effect of conspicuous pylons, buildings, tracks, car parks, snow fences and other facilities in an open hill landscape, rather than vegetation damage and soil erosion, serious though the latter may often be. This visual intrusion could be reduced by changes in management (ASH 1986; Watson 1988c), but even so the main effect would still be there. This is the chief reason why most hill walkers and other hill users have objected to proposed ski developments in the Northern Corries, which are of high value to them, but have not objected to ski developments at Coire Cas, Coire na Ciste, Glencoe, Glenshee Ski Centre, and the Lecht, or to proposed developments at Drumochter, Aonach Mor, Ben Wyvis, and Coire Laogh Mor on Cairn Gorm, which were not or are not of high value to them.

Bulldozed hill tracks

In terms of the number of hills and glens affected, the bulldozing of hill tracks for sporting purposes has been the most prevalent recent feature reducing the wild qualities of the Cairngorms. From the early 1960s, nearly all landowners in the area bulldozed tracks on open hill ground to give easier access for the shooting of deer and grouse (Watson 1974, 1984c). Most of these tracks were made cheaply, with inadequate drains, and with spoil and boulders dumped in heaps at the side. Many were conspicuous scars on hillsides, and some were clearly visible up to 30 kilometres away. As old footpaths tended to take good, well-drained lines, many tracks were bulldozed along these footpaths, which thereby became obliterated; these included popular rights of way along former historic drove routes. One track was bulldozed up to 1000 metres on Beinn a' Bhuird. When Mar Lodge Estate sought to bulldoze tracks into the National Nature Reserve at Glen Derry, Glen Geusachan and Glen Dee, the Nature Conservancy refused permission and the tracks were not made. However, on Glenfeshie Estate the NC allowed several tracks to be bulldozed inside the National Nature Reserve up the old drove route on the east bank of the River Feshie and up to over 900 metres in the arctic-alpine zone on the Moine Mhor. On several estates, bulldozed tracks went up to high plateaux where vehicles left the tracks and roamed over the short vegetation, causing vegetation damage that has lasted for years. Motor bicycles have followed, as well as unauthorised use of some tracks by tourists' vehicles.

Because of the bulldozed tracks, the size of roadless wild areas declined greatly (Watson 1984c). A survey including more than Grampian Region but not all of the 1967 'Cairngorm Area' showed that areas more than two miles (3.2 kilometres) from the nearest road or track decreased from 678 square kilometres in 1960 to 154 square kilometres in 1982, and the largest area of roadless terrain in 1960 had split into three separate parts by 1982.

Conservation groups and hill walkers argued that such tracks should be brought under planning controls. Regulations were brought in during 1980, stating that landowners now had to seek planning permission from the local authority if they wished to make new hill tracks above 300 metres altitude within National Scenic Areas designated by the Countryside Commission for Scotland. Since then, however, landowners at Glen Feshie and Glen Ey have made new tracks above 300 metres altitude inside National Scenic Areas, without seeking planning permission (Caufield 1985). When hill walkers complained to the respective District Councils, the Councils asked the landowners to seek 'retrospective planning permission', which they were granted. Inside the Cairngorms National Nature Reserve, Rothiemurchus Estate tried unsuccessfully to bulldoze a collapsed track in Gleann Einich in 1981, causing more erosion, and bulldozed an old track within the pine forest in 1984.

Muirburn

Muirburn for deer is done to provide a fresh young bite. On the moorland zone in the deer forests of the Cairngorms, as on deer forests in Scotland generally, muirburn fires have traditionally been large. This has continued since 1940. The fires frequently extend to fifty hectares and occasionally more than one square kilometre. Usually they are poorly controlled, and sometimes uncontrolled. Ground conditions are often too dry, resulting in hot fires that burn some of the soil and lead to soil erosion and very slow recovery of vegetation. This type of burning with large fires occurs on all deer forests in the area. An exception is the open hill owned by the Forestry Commission and the Highlands and Islands Development Board in Glen More, where no muirburn has been done since the late 1940s, but this case is unusual in that hardly any red deer have occurred there.

On grouse moors and on those parts of the deer forests where grouse are important in the estates' economies, muirburn has traditionally been practised in narrow strips, a kind of management which leads to higher grouse stocks. The fires are seldom too hot, and the risk of erosion is less because the burned patches are small. Nevertheless, muirburn fires on grouse moors have generally become bigger, on some moors due to fewer gamekeepers being employed.

Game preservation

Gamekeepers on grouse moors have for long killed birds and mammals that prey on grouse. On many grouse moors in the Cairngorms area, persecution by gamekeepers has prevented golden eagles from nesting regularly, and the number of pairs has decreased greatly since 1945 (Nethersole-Thompson & Watson 1981; Watson, Payne & Rae 1989). Hen harriers are often persecuted on grouse moors, many common buzzards have been shot, trapped or poisoned in Speyside (Picozzi & Weir 1976), and several golden eagles have been found dead from poisoning. Recently, it has been suggested that protection of birds of prey in Britain may have to be lifted in the interests of grouse shooting (Collins 1988). However, there is no evidence to justify this. Indeed, the evidence from the recent large general rise in grouse numbers over most parts of Scotland, including the Cairngorms, firmly rejects any suggestions that more predators are keeping grouse numbers generally at low trough levels (Moss & Watson 1989). Average grouse stocks over the years have been lower on some moors in the Cairngorms than they might have been, but the main reason for this is poor land management, involving large fires and overbrowsing of heather by high numbers of red deer and sheep. Average stocks of grouse have remained high in this area if land management for grouse has been efficient, as at Inchrory.

Afforestation of moorland and forest edge

Coniferous trees have been planted densely on open moorland in many places in and around the Cairngorms massif, usually including exotic species and often consisting mostly or entirely of exotic trees. On several deer forests, blocks of a size generally regarded by foresters as too small to be economic for timber production have been deer-fenced and planted, aided by public subsidy. According to local staff, the aim is to open them up for deer shelter as soon as possible.

Furthermore, dense coniferous plantations have been established close to or amongst scattered Old Caledonian pines or old birches on private land at Glen Lui, Glen Quoich, Dubh Ghleann, Invercauld, Balmoral, Little Inverey, Morrone, Abernethy, Rothiemurchus and Glen Feshie, including exotic conifers at Glen Lui, Glen Quoich, Dubh Ghleann and Glen Feshie, and on the Forestry Commission's land at Glen More and Invereshie. In the Cairngorms National Nature Reserve at Glen Luibeg, the Nature Conservancy in the 1950s fenced off an area of moorland that contained widely scattered Old Caledonian pines. Inside the fence many pine seedlings then regenerated naturally. This was enough to extend the forest, given the long life-span of Scots pines, but the Conservancy later planted up the enclosure (Watson 1983). About 1971 the Forestry Commission ploughed and planted inside a fenced enclosure high on Cairn Gorm, on an exposed ridge where these developments formed a conspicuous intrusion on the open hill landscape. In 1982, a moorland hillside inside the NNR above Achlean in Glen Feshie was fenced, ploughed and planted densely with Scots pines, aided by funds from NCC. The hillside lay between two areas of Old Caledonian pines, and small numbers of pines were regenerating naturally on it before the fence was erected.

High numbers of red deer

On most deer forests in the area, numerous red deer have for decades prevented woodland from spreading back on to the nearby moorland; they eat the seedlings as soon as these appear above the ground vegetation. The area's potential for trees can be judged by the many coniferous and hardwood trees that grow on cliffs inaccessible to deer. Obviously, good regeneration will occur only if deer are fenced out or their numbers reduced. If natural forest processes are considered important, as is usually the case in nature reserves and equivalent protected areas internationally, then deer numbers would have to be cut. Provided that tree regeneration is monitored, all that would be required is for the deer cull to be increased to a point where enough regeneration was judged to be occurring. 'Enough' here means the amount needed to maintain and extend the natural forest and its composition of different tree species over decades, not the amount that a forester would seek from a wood whose main purpose was timber production.

High deer densities have led to an increase of bare ground on some low ground on Glen Feshie, Mar Lodge estate and Invercauld. Deer numbers in the east Highlands have increased greatly since the 1960s (Red Deer Commission 1987). On low ground with high numbers of wintering deer in Atholl, Mar, Invercauld, and Glen Feshie, heather is cropped close to ground level in places (Nethersole-Thompson & Watson 1981). As a result, average grouse stocks have declined there, due to the shortage of tall heather for cover and the replacement of heather by grass after burning (Watson & Moss 1987).

Moorland reverting to forest

On certain lower parts of the Cairngorms area, much moorland has been reverting towards forest by natural regeneration (Watson 1966; Nethersole-Thompson & Watson 1981; Watson & Hinge 1989). The main areas for this are in mid Deeside and Strath Don, and to a lesser extent at Dorback and near Tomintoul. These areas are outside the range of high stocks of red deer, and are characterised by less muirburn and by fewer sheep and cattle on the hill. The fewer sheep and cattle are a result of the rundown of many arable hill farms and their conversion to pasture, whose carrying capacity for winter keep is low. The main trees coming in are Scots pines, but birches predominate in some places, and several other native tree species have appeared. There has been no immediate financial incentive for landowners to allow such pine regeneration to continue and spread. Instead, immediate grants have been available for fencing, ploughing and dense planting, which result in destruction of the developing natural woodland. Several cases of such destruction by intensive afforestation have occurred in the area, including ground inside the Muir of Dinnet National Nature Reserve after the reserve was declared. Elsewhere, some gamekeepers have burned regenerating pine seedlings in big fires and have chopped down larger trees, so as to keep the ground open as heather moorland.

A special case of moorland changing towards forest and scrub is on Cairn Gorm and the Northern Corries SSSI, where thousands of Scots pines and some trees of other species have spread upwards from the Old Caledonian forest edge on Rothiemurchus and Glen More (Watson 1981; Miller 1986). Many red deer formerly summered on Cairn Gorm and the plateau, and wintered mainly in the woods of Glen More. After the Forestry Commission fenced off the woods in the mid 1940s, the herd disappeared in the early 1950s, some years before the big increase of visitors that followed the building of the public road and chairlifts on Cairn Gorm. Muirburn also stopped. Tree regeneration then increased, and the scattered trees spread up to a potential tree line, where the trees at higher altitude are mere scrub because of severe exposure. This change is of great interest in demonstrating the artificial nature of much of the treeless and scrubless moorland in the Cairngorms, and in showing the effects of browsing.

Glen Muick and Lochnagar Wildlife Reserve

The Scottish Wildlife Trust and Balmoral Estate declared their reserve agreement in 1974. Much publicity followed, and visitors increased rapidly, leading in turn to footpath damage, more litter, and more signs and regulations. The relative freedom that climbers had previously experienced when they camped in this area became curtailed. Despite the Reserve designation, the promoters of a Jubilee bonfire on Lochnagar were allowed to proceed with their plans. Tons of old tyres and other rubbish were lifted to the summit by a helicopter. A snowstorm prevented the Jubilee bonfire from taking place, but the rubbish was later burned so that it would not have to be taken down again.

The 'honeypot' idea

Part of the 'honeypot' idea for recreation is that attractive facilities for the public at a few well promoted, heavily visited places will give many people the benefits of recreation there. The other part of the idea is that this should relieve pressures on the wider and often more outstanding countryside round about, and so should benefit hill walkers and others who prefer wild country. Cramond (this book) describes the idea in more detail, using as examples the visitor centre of the National Trust for Scotland at Ben Lawers, and the HIDB's Cairngorm Estate. Some regard the visitor centre at Glen Muick Reserve as another example.

What happened at Glen Muick Reserve is a local example of a principle well known from abroad, that strong promotion of an area often leads to heavy use. If the area is on fertile soils at low altitudes, the ground may well be able to cope. If it is on poor soils at high altitudes, however, heavy use leads to damage which cannot be repaired without recourse to techniques that detract from a wild area. When a visitor centre at Glen Muick was first suggested, a few people suggested that it should be beside a public through-road on sheltered, fertile ground down the glen or down by the River Dee, and not at a road end at the top of a glen, where over-use of the ground would be likely.

Cramond's idea (this book) is to use Cairn Gorm as a well-managed honeypot for many tourists to enjoy. He suggests that this would relieve pressures on the National Nature Reserve and the Northern Corries SSSI. However, the infertile, highly erodible granite soils, sparse vegetation cover and severe climate of Cairn Gorm make it inherently unsuitable for a honeypot, because the ground is so easily damaged by even low human pressures. Moreover, the honeypot which is already at Cairn Gorm has not relieved pressures on the NNR and the Northern Corries, but has added to them through the easy access provided by the chairlift and public road to Coire Cas (Watson 1967, 1981; Morris, Hammond & Kessler 1974; Anderson Semens Houston 1981).

Organised parties and mass events

These have taken place for decades, but have become more frequent in recent years and led to conflict in 1987. Inside National Nature Reserves, helicopters have been used unnecessarily (Nethersole-Thompson & Watson 1981) for courses in mountain training from Glenmore Lodge, for off-piste skiers, and for other parties. There have been sponsored walks with hundreds of people at a time through Lairig Ghru, Capel Mount and Tolmount, organised by mountain rescue teams and other bodies. On midsummer night in 1987, a hundred walkers went to the top of Ben Macdui for the Cairngorm Club's centenary celebration. Such events damage paths and detract from the wilderness experience of other walkers. Increasingly, mountaineers are stating that, no matter how good the cause may be, the end does not justify such means (e.g. Gordon 1987).

Chief conclusions

1.   The main human impacts on the Cairngorms environment above timber line occurred in previous centuries, but the number and scale of new forms of impact have increased rapidly since 1940. Previous impacts caused little decline in the area's wild qualities, but recent impacts have reduced these qualities considerably.

2.   Because these qualities have declined, it follows that the conservation designations of NNR, SSSI and National Scenic Area have not given strong enough protection.

3.   Many organisations with different and often conflicting aims have responsibility for the Cairngorms, and no one body has predominance. The inevitable result is increasing, continual conflict. Many different individuals and organisations own the Cairngorms area. Understandably the private owners wish to use their land in their own way for their own main purposes, and similarly the public owners. However, these purposes often conflict with national and international requirements for conservation. Standards or rules to maintain or enhance conservation values could be set and checked by a body such as NCC, and NCC could put forward a management plan at least for the Cairngorms NNR and nearby SSSIs. The regional staff of NCC did circulate a draft management plan for the NNR in the late 1970s, for comment by numerous organisations and individuals. Many people thought it a useful plan, but it was almost immediately withdrawn after a local landowner objected. No second version has appeared since.

4.   The ways in which public money is used have been at the root of many of the conflicts between development and conservation in the area. Ski developments have been subsidised through the building of new roads and

car parks, remedial works at them, road improvements, snow clearing, emergency evacuation, medical costs of skiing accidents, grants for tows and other equipment by public organisations in Britain and the EEC, and promotion of ski developments by several public bodies in Scotland. One bulldozed hill track that was subsequently used almost entirely for deer stalking was backed by agricultural grant, and a recent track bulldozed within the National Scenic Area at Glen Ey involved an application for agricultural grant. Other tracks that were bulldozed mainly or partly outside areas to be afforested have been grant-aided for forestry. Subsidised intensive afforestation has led to the most frequent and widespread declines in the wild qualities of the lower moorlands in recent decades. In many places this destroyed or reduced natural tree regeneration that was turning moorland into native woodland without cost to the taxpayer. Critics suggest that public money for afforestation in areas such as the Cairngorms should be put instead into natural tree regeneration which would enhance wildlife and landscape, and so benefit tourism and local employment (e.g. Royal Society for the Protection of Birds 1982; Countryside Commission for Scotland 1986; Callander 1988).

5. Experience from abroad shows that Nature Reserves or other conservation designations do not work well unless they are seen to benefit the local community.

REFERENCES

AITKEN, R. (1985). *Scottish Mountain Footpaths.* Countryside Commission for Scotland, Perth.

ANDERSON SEMENS HOUSTON (1981). *Environmental Impact Analysis. Proposed Expansion of Downhill Skiing Facilities Coire an t'Sneachda, Coire an Lochan and Lurchers Gully, Cairngorm.* ASH Environmental Design Partnership, Glasgow.

ASH ENVIRONMENTAL DESIGN PARTNERSHIP (1986). *Environmental Design of Ski Areas in Scotland. A Practical Handbook.* Report for the Countryside Commission for Scotland and Highland Regional Council. ASH Environmental Design Partnership, Glasgow.

BAYFIELD, N.G. (1971). Some effects of walking and ski-ing on vegetation at Cairngorm. *Symposia of the British Ecological Society,* **11**, 469-485.

BAYFIELD, N.G. (1973). Use and deterioration of unmanaged Scottish hill paths. *Journal of Applied Ecology,* **10**, 639-648.

BAYFIELD, N.G. (1974). Burial of vegetation by erosion debris near ski lifts on Cairngorm, Scotland. *Biological Conservation,* **6**, 246-251.

BAYFIELD, N.G., URQUHART, U.H. & COOPER, S.M. (1981). Susceptibility of four species of *Cladonia* to disturbance by trampling in the Cairngorm mountains of Scotland. *Journal of Applied Ecology,* **18**, 303-310.

BIRKS, H.H. (1970). Studies in the vegetational history of Scotland. I. A pollen diagram from Abernethy Forest, Inverness-shire. *Journal of Ecology,* **58**, 827-846.

CALLANDER, R.F. (1987). *A Pattern of Landownership in Scotland.* Haughend Publications, Finzean, Aberdeenshire.

CALLANDER, R.F. (1988). Forestry for rural Scotland. The BANC Report. *Forests for Britain,* pp. 40-49. Packard Publishing, Funtington, Chichester.

CAUFIELD, C. (1985). Setbacks for conservation in Highlands. *New Scientist,* 3 January, p. 6.

COLLINS, P. (1988). Return of the grouse. *Insight,* spring 1988, 38-40.

COUNTRYSIDE COMMISSION FOR SCOTLAND (1986). *Forestry in Scotland.* Countryside Commission for Scotland, Battleby, Perth.

DARLING, F.F. (1947). *Natural History in the Highlands and Islands,* Collins, London.

DARLING, F.F. & BOYD, J.M. (1969). *The Highlands and Islands,* 2nd ed. Collins, London.

GILMORE, D. (1975). *Recreation – its Impact and Management in the Northern Cairngorms.* Unpublished MSc thesis, Unviersity College, London.

GLENSHEE CHAIRLIFT COMPANY (1987). *Development and Management Plan for Glenshee Ski Centre 1987-1991.* Glenshee Chairlift Company, Braemar.

GORDON, A. (1987). Mass events in the hills – are they appropriate? Spring newsletter, 20-21. North East Mountain Trust, Aberdeen.

LECHT SKI COMPANY (1986). *Development and Management Plan.* Lecht Ski Company, Strathdon.

MILLER, G.R. (1986). *Development of Subalpine Scrub at Northern Corries, Cairngorms SSSI.* Institute of Terrestrial Ecology, Banchory.

MILSOM, T.P. & WATSON, A. (1984). Numbers and spacing of summering snow buntings and snow cover in the Cairngorms. *Scottish Birds,* **13**, 19-23.

80

MORRIS, D., HAMMOND, E.C. & KESSLER, C.D.J. (1974). *Cairngorms National Nature Reserve. A Report on the Characteristics of Visitor Use.* Nature Conservancy Council, Aviemore.

MOSS, R. & WATSON, A. (1989). Red grouse update. *Shooting Times,* June 16, 26-27.

NETHERSOLE-THOMPSON, D. (1952). *Survey of the Birds of Rothiemurchus Forest and Western Cairngorms.* Report to the Royal Society for the Protection of Birds and the Nature Conservancy.

NETHERSOLE-THOMPSON, D. & WATSON, A. (1981). *The Cairngorms.* Melven Press, Perth.

O'SULLIVAN, P.E. (1976). Pollen analysis and radiocarbon-dating of a core from Loch Pityoulish, East-central Highlands of Scotland. *Journal of Biogeography,* **3**, 293-302.

PICOZZI, N. & WEIR, D. (1976). Dispersal and causes of death of buzzards. *British Birds,* **69**, 193-201.

RED DEER COMMISSION (1987). *Annual Report 1986.* HMSO, Edinburgh.

RENNIE, F. (1986). The role of conservation in Highland landuse. *Land Ownership and Use* (ed. by J. Hulbert), pp. 20-28. Fletcher Paper No. 2, Andrew Fletcher Society, Edinburgh.

RITCHIE, J. (1920). *The Influence of Man on Animal Life in Scotland.* Cambridge University Press, Cambridge.

ROYAL SOCIETY FOR THE PROTECTION OF BIRDS (1982). *The Conservation of Britain's Native Pinewoods – A Discussion Paper,* pp. 1-9, RSPB, Edinburgh.

STEWART, D. (1986). *Roads in Hills and Mountains.* North East Mountain Trust, Aberdeen.

WATSON, A. (1966). Hill birds of the Cairngorms. *Scottish Birds,* **4**, 179-203.

WATSON, A. (1967). Public pressures on soils, plants and animals near ski lifts in the Cairngorms. *The Biotic Effects of Public Pressures on the Environment* (ed. by E. Duffey), pp. 38-45. Natural Environment Research Council, London.

WATSON, A. (1974). The vanishing wilderness. *Mountain Life,* **11**, 18-19.

WATSON, A. (1977). Wildlife potential in the Cairngorms region. *Scottish Birds,* **9**, 245-266.

WATSON, A. (1979). Bird and mammal numbers in relation to human impact at ski lifts on Scottish hills. *Journal of Applied Ecology,* **16**, 753-764.

WATSON, A. (1981). *Detailed Analysis,* Mimeographed evidence lodged with Scottish Development Department, Edinburgh, for Lurcher's Gully Public Inquiry, Kingussie.

WATSON, A. (1982). Effects of human impact on ptarmigan and red grouse near ski lifts in Scotland. *Annual Report of the Institute of Terrestrial Ecology,* 51. Cambridge.

WATSON, A. (1983). Eighteenth century deer numbers and pine regeneration near Braemar, Scotland. *Biological Conservation,* **25**, 289-305.

WATSON, A. (1984a). Wilderness values and threats to wilderness in the Cairngorms. *Wilderness: the Way Ahead* (ed. by M. Inglis & V. Martin), pp. 262-267. Findhorn Publications, Forres.

WATSON, A. (1984b). Paths and people in the Cairngorms. *Scottish Geographical Magazine,* **100**, 151-160.

WATSON, A. (1984c). A survey of vehicular hill tracks in north-east Scotland for land use planning. *Journal of Environmental Management,* **18**, 345-353.

WATSON, A. (1985). Soil erosion and vegetation damage near ski lifts at Cairn Gorm, Scotland. *Biological Conservation,* **33**, 363-381.

WATSON, A. (1988a). Decline of the wild. *Cairngorms at the Crossroads* (ed. by J. Crumley), pp. 8-13. Scottish Wild Land Group, Edinburgh.

WATSON, A. (1988b). Dotterel *Charadrius morinellus* numbers in relation to human impact in Scotland. *Biological Conservation,* **43**, 245-256.

WATSON, A. (1988c). *Environmental Baseline Study – Glenshee Ski Centre 1987.* Institute of Terrestrial Ecology, Banchory.

WATSON, A. (1989). *Ground Disturbance, Soil Erosion and Vegetation Damage at Cairn Gorm in 1988 compared with 1981.* Institute of Terrestrial Ecology, Banchory.

WATSON, A. (in press). Changes in land condition after ski developments at Cairn Gorm. *The Glen More Forest Park* (ed. by J.W.H. Conroy). North East Mountain Trust, Aberdeen.

WATSON, A. (in press). Outstanding wildlife in Glen More Forest Park. *The Glen More Forest Park* (ed. by J.W.H. Conroy). North East Mountain Trust, Aberdeen.

WATSON, A. & ALLAN, E. (1986). Papers relating to game poaching on Deeside, 1766-1832. *Northern Scotland,* **7**, 39-45.

WATSON, A. & DUFF, J. (1972). Lessons to youth parties from the Feith Buidhe Disaster. *Climber & Rambler,* **12**, 282-287.

WATSON, A. & HINGE, M. (1989). *Natural Tree Regeneration on Open Upland in Deeside and Donside.* Institute of Terrestrial Ecology, Banchory.

WATSON, A. & LEITCH, A. (1987). *Lecht Monitoring Autumn 1987.* Institute of Terrestrial Ecology, banchory.

WATSON, A. & MOSS, R. (1987). Scottish grouse. *Shooting Times,* 4470, 21-22.

WATSON, A., PAYNE, S. & RAE, R. (1989). Golden Eagles *Aquila chrysaetos:* land use and food in northeast Scotland. *Ibis,* **131**, 336-348.

WATSON, A. & WATSON, R.D. (1983a). *Tourism, Land Use and Rural Communities in Mountain Areas. The Swiss Approach and its Relevance for Scotland.* Report for Grampian Regional Council, Aberdeen.

WATSON, A. & WATSON, R.D. (1983b). *The Lecht Ski Development. The Impact on Soils and Vegetation and Recommendations for its Amelioration.* Report for Grampian Regional Council, Aberdeen.

WATSON, A. & WATSON, R.D. (1986). Scottish landholding and its social and cultural aspects compared with Swiss and Scandinavian. *Land Ownership and Use* (ed. by J. Hulbert), pp. 12-19. Fletcher Paper No. 2, Andrew Fletcher Society, Edinburgh.

Beinn Mheadhoin from the cairn of Beinn a' Chaorrainn. *The wilderness and stark beauty of winter in the Cairngorms. (Nick Picozzi)*

Loch Avon and the Shelter Stone Crag. *Loch Avon, the largest loch in Scotland above 2000 ft, cuts deep into the heart of the Cairngorms. (Dave Gowans)*

The Old Caledonian forest. *Old pines with regenerating young trees, home to many interesting plants and animals, and an important part of the scenery. (Drennan Watson)*

Red deer stags cooling off in the river Feshie.
Red deer are very common in the Caledonian forest, and often eat all young trees, as seen here. (Dave Gowans)

Bulldozed tracks in Glen Ey. *The proliferation of bulldozed tracks over the past 20 years has greatly reduced the area of wildness. (Jim Conroy)*

The telltale signs of a big fire. *Burning wide expanses on steep slopes leads to erosion and is all too common in the area. (Adam Watson)*

Regenerating birch woods. Birch woods extend from the valley farms to the high glens. Like the Caledonian pines, they often show little regeneration, but on the National Nature Reserve at Dinnet there is vigorous regeneration. (Jim Conroy)

Moss Campion (Silene acaulis) This plant, typical of exposed gravels on the plateau, adds a splash of colour. (Nick Picozzi)

Astragalus alpinus. *(Nick Picozzi)*

Dryas octopetala *(Drennan Watson)*

Two of the many rare plants of the Cairngorms

88

Downhill skiing on Cairn Gorm. *Cairn Gorm attracts many thousands each winter to ski on its slopes. From the ski area there is a fine view across Strath Spey towards the north-west Highlands. (Steve Bateson)*

Lochnagar. *Dark Lochnagar of song and story. These spectacular crags have introduced many to climbing. (Jim Conroy)*

Mountain burns. *Heavy rain and sudden thaws can quickly change them into raging torrents. (Jim Conroy)*

The dotterel. *One of the rarer British breeding species. (Dave Gowans)*

Derry Cairngorm and Glen Derry. *Glen Derry traversed by one of the old drove roads across the Cairngorms, has a magnificent tract of old Caledonian forest. (Nick Picozzi)*

The tranquillity and wildness of the high mountains.
A summer dawn above Loch Etchachan. (Adam Watson)

A HILLMAN LOOKS AT THE CONSERVATION OF THE CAIRNGORMS

R. DRENNAN WATSON

North East Mountain Trust, Brig o Lead, Alford, Aberdeenshire AB3 8PD

SUMMARY

1. When all features valued in mountains are considered, the Cairngorms are clearly Britain's premier mountain range. The reasons for this are:

   a. their scale;

   b. their concentration of high ground;

   c. their diversity of terrain;

   d. their varied and distinctive wildlife;

   e. the wide range of recreational opportunities that they offer in their moorlands, foothills, and the central core of major peaks and high plateaux;

   f. their value as a wilderness area.

2. Over a long period, but especially in recent years, the natural and recreational values have been successively degraded.

3. Some remnants of the Old Caledonian pine forest and birch woods have been destroyed and most remnants damaged by felling, muirburn, ploughing for planting, and above all overgrazing by red deer.

4. Bulldozed tracks, often poorly made, have greatly reduced the area of remote country.

5. Uncontrolled muirburn has damaged sensitive soils and vegetation.

6. In the Northern Cairngorms new roads, tourist development and all-year use of the Coire Cas chairlift have given mass access to the most sensitive areas, causing damage to spread into the most valuable part of the Cairngorms National Nature Reserve.

7. Protective designations, including NNRs, SSSIs, NPDAs and NSAs, intended to protect the area, have been largely ineffective or even damaging.

8. The future values of the Cairngorms can be assured only if the many people who have benefited from them are willing to put something back.

9. The choice for the future protection of the Cairngorms must be made between purchase or planning.

10. If faith is to be put in planning, future protective measures must be restorative and rigorously effective, must recognise the potential of the Cairngorms as wild country, and must meet the minimum management aims defined in the *Future of the Cairngorms* (1982).

INTRODUCTION

It is well over thirty years since I stood with a friend on the Inverey road on a fine June evening and gazed across the Dee to new hills. On this first visit to the Cairngorms, of which I had heard so much, the rounded, rolling foothills which we looked up to did not immediately impress callow youths weaned on the sharp Sisters of Kintail and the steep gullies of Glencoe, but that soon changed.

The direct approach in all things to do with mountains was something we much favoured, and that meant a beeline for the Linn of Quoich to rendezvous with our mates. We scrambled down the grassy bank where the clear shimmering Dee curved close to the road, and forded. It was deeper and colder than expected. But we were "lang-legget loons", and held our ex-army boots on top of our ex-army rucksacks on our heads with one hand, and lifted our kilts with the other. On the far bank, we lay chilled but dry, and warmed out on the grass.

Before us lay the meadows of the Dee, turning golden in the evening sun. As we wandered across them through this blissfully peaceful scene, we came suddenly on a dramatic encounter. First we noticed the odd stag stirring among the scattered, ageing birches, then groups of deer appeared moving restively in little panics, and then a flood of them with drumming hooves, like a river of brown. One large herd, then another, then another, surged round us bunching, merging, spreading out and merging again. Finally, in a great herd, they swung facing us in a long line of hundreds and thundered towards us. We were rivetted, but a hundred yards from us the stags stopped stock still, gazed as we did at them, then charged off across the broad meadows.

Our next experience was silent and more stately, but just as impressive. We neared the river Quoich and came among the ancient pines, now flooded and russet in the light of the dipping sun. We trod silently on the pine needles, looking all about, put down our rucksacks and explored deeper among the trees. They stood immense; their richness of character and colour, their grandeur, their sense of age, all impressed us. How could anything so silent say so much? To this day, I have never seen, anywhere in the world, trees more striking and fascinating than these ancient Scots pines of Caledon.

This was a good place! We settled close by the Quoich, pitched our tent, and cooked tea.

Next day we wandered for miles through these magnificent pines up a track that soon became a footpath, then disappeared and, rendered weary by our failure to bring a good lunch, had a hard trek through that trackless, wild country, to make our first Cairngorms ascent – Beinn a' Bhuird.

That night the deer, heads and antlers silhouetted in the light of a full moon, picked their way down through the ancient pines to barely twenty yards from the fire and gazed warily at us.

On the morrow, a scorching Sunday, we bathed in the crystal waters of the Punchbowl of the Quoich. Then, like trusties returning to prison, we set off for grimy Glasgow again.

I relate this tale at length for several reasons. It contains so much of the best of what the Cairngorms then had to offer: impressive wildlife, beautiful scenery, challenge, and travel in remote country. Also, the value of such experiences, especially when you are young, is inestimable. They are never forgotten, and for many people change forever their attitude to wildlife and scenery, and spin enduring bonds of attachment between them and their native land. Lastly, it permits me to examine in this paper how much of that experience a young person of my age then could have today, or will be able to have in another thirty years if present trends continue.

I will attempt to do this by explaining first what particular values the Cairngorms have to offer, then examine what is happening to these assets, and lastly offer some few thoughts on the future.

THE VALUES OF THE CAIRNGORMS

In our booklet *The Future of the Cairngorms* (1982) Kai Curry-Lindahl, Adam Watson, and I stated, 'The Cairngorms are Britain's premier mountain range'. (Curry-Lindahl, Watson & Watson 1982). This was a bold claim, especially in the face of so many enthusiasts, each with his or her own favourite mountains. Certainly one can point to features, such as spectacular ridges, where other Scottish ranges would score much higher, but it is when you make the comparison across all mountain features that the Cairngorms stand pre-eminent.

The diversity and distinctive qualities of the terrain

Diversity is not a word that many would at first apply to the Cairngorms. First impressions can be the opposite – a relative uniformity in shape and mould that contrasts sharply with the diversity of silhouette, of for example the Torridon mountains of Liathach, Beinn Eighe, and Beinn Alligin. But more prolonged thought gives a different perspective. It is a result mainly of a combination of their scale and the concentration of very high ground (in British terms) that they contain. W.H.Murray (1989), as might be expected, has described their distinctive landscape qualities within the Highland scene better than any, saying:

> In 1961 I made a survey of Highland landscape for the National Trust for Scotland, when I compared fifty-two Highland regions one with another. I found that among all these the High Cairngorms had a unique landscape quality. At long distance they might seem to the casual glance to lack distinctive shape, but a penetration to the interior removes that impression. Great corries have been carved into their eastern and northern faces. In some, dark lochans are ringed by cliffs; in others, bare moorlands sweep up to craggy skylines, drawing the eyes over the Cairngorm massif. Nowhere outside Skye can such a variety be seen within a like area. The wastes of shattered stone on the summit plateaux form the biggest area of high ground in Britain. Their appeal is not an obvious one. In the act of exploring them the immense scale on which the scene is set is gradually revealed. This, with the vast corries, the massive slopes, the long passes, the wide skies, and the very bareness of the ground, where the elements work with a power not known at lower altitudes, gives to these plateaux their distinctive quality.

Having been little affected by the main ice sheet, the plateaux remain largely untouched by glaciation. Their landscape comes from more ancient times, before even there were mountains. I have always found it amazing to stand looking at the tors on Ben Avon and consider that they are probably far older than Ben Avon itself. Although the climate of the high plateaux is subarctic, it is also affected by the relative closeness of the Atlantic. Mountains with such a subarctic-oceanic climate are rare in the world.

It is this combination of high-level plateaux, subarctic and oceanic climate, and preglacial landscape, along with the beautifully adapted wildlife that this supports, which gives the plateaux their high wildlife and scientific value.

The diversity and distinctive qualities of the wildlife

The changes in climate that occur over the range of altitude from sea level to summit cause a gradation in both landscape and wildlife that produces much of the diversity of scenery and wildlife which we enjoy on a mountain day. The Cairngorms do not harbour any species that are unique to them. However, because of their great average height in British terms, the concentration of high ground that they contain, the quality of the surrounding moorlands, and the fragments of Old Caledonian pine forest that they harbour, they contain the finest assemblage of plants and wildlife of any Scottish mountain range. When Kai Curry-Lindahl surveyed the National Parks and Nature Reserves of north-west Europe for the International Union for the Conservation of Nature and Natural Resources (IUCN), he ranked the Cairngorms as Britain's foremost conservation area (Curry-Lindahl 1974). To many hill users this scientific value of the wildlife may be of little direct importance, but the contribution of wildlife to the experience of the whole day is considerable.

Range of recreational opportunity

The diversity of activities commonly pursued in these mountains has expanded since the days of our chilly crossing of the Dee. Rock and ice climbing, hill walking, wild camping, backpacking, and the study of natural history have not only increased greatly in popularity, but have been joined by ski mountaineering, cross-country and downhill skiing. The Cairngorms give greater scope to a greater range of these activities than any other British range. As we stated in our booklet (Curry-Lindahl *et al.* 1982):

> We have here the largest area of high level hill walking in Britain, four of the five highest mountains, the most famous and challenging hill passes, and the best places for the rapidly growing sport of ski touring. The spectacular corries offer magnificent scenery and some of Britain's best ice, snow and rock climbing on scores of fine granite crags.

As testimony to the opportunities that the Cairngorms offer for these sports, we went on to point out how:

> Modern mountaineering techniques of ice-climbing and winter route assessment, which developed first in the Cairngorms, have since evolved and become widely used abroad. The massif has also been the training ground for mountaineers who have made outstanding contributions to the sport internationally, for noted arctic explorers, and for military units training for operations in harsh conditions.

The Cairngorms are also better adapted to cross country skiing and ski mountaineering than any other British range due to their climate, the large area of high ground that they contain, and the more level rolling nature of the extensive high plateaux. In addition, journeys on foot lasting several days allow one to enjoy the wild country.

Diversity of recreational opportunity in the different parts of the Cairngorms

The Cairngorms can be divided into three main areas, the moorland, foothills and high tops. Each of the three has distinctive patterns of recreation.

In the core are the main mountain tops – not distinct peaks connected narrowly by shoulders and ridges, or isolated bens as in Sutherland and the west – but groups of almost minor hills rising gently from high plateaux, of which the Cairn Gorm-Ben Macdui plateau is the classic example. Foothills which form the approaches to most mountain ranges in the world are not really a feature of most of Scotland's mountain areas. They tend to rise from the road, often at sea level, straight to their summits. This is a major reason why the Scottish scenery, with such relatively small mountains, can be so spectacular. By contrast, the Cairngorms are surrounded by foothills to a much greater extent than any other British range, and this has implications for their recreational value.

Below the foothills of the Cairngorms lies another type of country which many Scots regard as commonplace but has great recreational and wildlife value – heather moorland. Heather moorland of any appreciable size is comparatively rare now in European and world terms, and the eastern and central Highlands of Scotland contain some of the better extensive examples. It is mostly a man-made habitat, divested of its natural forest by tree felling, and kept in a largely treeless state by grazing and burning. In a sense it is a degraded habitat. However, its domination by a rich mixture of semi-natural vegetation of heather, bracken, grass and moss, give it a scenic mixture of subtle hues at any time of the year. In the natural conditions of Scotland, many animal species evolved to inhabit the extensive open land above the treeline, and the less extensive open patches that occurred within the forested areas below. When the treeless open moorlands were created, they too were colonised by many of the species from the open areas above and below, giving a wide range of wildlife easily visible to walkers and others.

Because the Cairngorms were too infertile to support much agriculture, they remained relatively uncontaminated when problems, such as DDT pollution, were widespread elsewhere. As a result, these large moorland areas formed important reservoirs of relatively uncontaminated wildlife such as peregrine falcons and golden eagles when they bred poorly or became scarce elsewhere.

The moorlands of the Cairngorms thus form an extensive area of rich landscape and wildlife value. Increasingly many walkers and cross-country skiers who are not necessarily interested in ascending to the high plateaux make use of these moors.

The foothills of the Cairngorms share these values and have similar recreational uses. In the foothills lies some of the best country for walking and good cross-country skiing in Scotland. In places they offer an added dimension of long, ice-deepened lochs which cut far into the hills. A major effect of the foothills is that feature of Cairngorms climbing, 'the long walk in'. Only in the Northern Cairngorms, at Glenmore, where access roads and the local absence of foothills have made access easy, is this approach missing, and the results of this to many are not desirable.

Amongst these foothills and moors are the remnants of the Old Caledonian pine forest, one of the most unusual and valuable assets of the Cairngorms. The boreal forest stretches far across the northern parts of Europe, Asia and North America and is part of the great band of coniferous-dominated forests known as the Taiga. The Caledonian forest is a remnant of the boreal forest. Little of this forest is left in western Europe in anything approaching its natural condition.

The fragments of the Caledonian forest found in Scotland and especially in the Cairngorms are not virgin. They have felt the axe many times, and been degraded by overgrazing and burning, but the trees are the direct descendants of those first colonisers that came in soon after the ice ages slackened their grip. These areas of ancient woodland have been more or less continuously under forest since then.

They can claim further distinction. The Scots pine is a very widespread conifer, occurring all the way from the western coast of Europe to Siberia. It is perhaps the world's most successful conifer. However, the form of forest it produced in Scotland, while being obviously related to some Scandinavian forests for example, is distinctly different and occurs nowhere else. The importance and uniqueness of these natural pine woods have been described in detail by Steven and Carlisle (1959).

The recreational, scenic and educational value of these ancient forest fragments, which have stood in these sites since soon after the retreat of the glaciers, is immense. They have an extraordinary atmosphere. You cannot really understand much of the story of Scotland until you have been in such a forest fragment and realise that this is the landscape in which much of it took place. They are a key part of Scottish history. As we stated in our booklet (Curry-Lindahl et al. 1982):

> But these aged forests are much more than that. The old trees have an individuality and beauty that makes them one of our best scenic attractions. The Old Caledonian forest is, further, a living part of our history. It is as much a part of our historical heritage as castles and cathedrals, and considerably more ancient, going back for 8,000 years. It is the primeval landscape from which most of our country evolved. Steven and Carlisle knew how much these forests conveyed of our origins

when they said in their classic text on the old woods, 'To stand in them is to feel the past'.

We cannot leave a discussion about the forests of the Cairngorms without mention of the birch woodlands. If the Scots pine was made to impress us, then the birch was made to charm us. Where the pine is stern and sturdy, the birch is delicate and subtle, giving an impression of fragility that belies its toughness. With its shapely hanging fronds, its silver bark and deep pink twigs strikingly exposed in winter, the marvellous spring flush of green leaves that cast a light shade in summer and turn to fiery autumn tints, there is not a season of the year when the silver birch does not give depth and charm to the landscape. In the pale northern light, its striking range of textures and hues are enhanced so that it enriches many an otherwise unremarkable scene. The common birch shares less of these visual attractions but in spring it perfumes the air of woodland walks.

A walk through a birchwood is one of the outstanding recreational experiences that the area has to offer. Both species of birch harbour a wide range of wildlife, and enrich the soil, unlike spruces which acidify and impoverish it. The birches provide good fuel and increasingly find a market as pulp.

Despite this wide range of virtues our birches have suffered grievously, chiefly through grazing and burning preventing regeneration and, in places, continued felling in the absence of regeneration. Many surviving birch woods have been underplanted with Sitka spruce, shading out the birch as they grow above it; eventually they destroy the birch wood. In some places, birch has regenerated where sheep grazing has been withdrawn or excluded, but over large areas, along with the other indigenous broadleaved species of the Cairngorms such as aspen and blackthorn, it has been reduced to a few shattered remnants of ageing decaying trees or stunted specimens sheltering secure from burning and grazing in deep gullies or the gorges of rivers.

At the heart of the Cairngorms lie the major summits with their corries, plateaux and high-level lochs, the largest area of land in Britain in near natural condition.

By Scottish standards, the corries are unusually large, containing spectacular and diverse arenas of cliffs, often bottomed by beautiful lochans. They are the setting for the rock and ice climbing of the range, climbs which end, not on ridges and isolated peaks, but on the high plateaux.

The recreational value of the high Cairngorms stems partly from the way the walker or skier, once on these plateaux, can range freely over large areas of this remarkable terrain, with unimpeded views of distant hills and spectacular glimpses across deep defiles and corries that were cut into the plateaux by glaciers.

The wilderness values of the Cairngorms

I use the word wilderness here deliberately, and am fully prepared to defend its use against those who would challenge the concept of true wilderness in Britain. Much of the confusion surrounding claims about wilderness areas in Scotland stems from the way different people define the word wilderness. 'Wilderness' can be applied to an area in an ecological sense, in which it means an area where the ecosystem with its indigenous plants and animals is still largely unmodified by man. It should be noted that man is an indigenous species in nearly all such wilderness areas outside of the Antarctic and some parts of the high Arctic, and has significant impact on them. Such areas can be scientifically defined on the map by study of the plant and animal species in them.

There is also the use of the word 'wilderness' to describe an area that gives people a certain experience. In our times, a major goal of the recreation of increasing numbers of people is to experience just such a sense of wilderness. There are two major elements in such an experience.

1.   A sense of closeness and intensity of exposure to nature. This seems to result when an individual is alone, or relatively alone, in country lacking and distant from any human artifacts such as houses or roads. It is strongest in places where natural forces have produced dramatic effects like the great spectacular corries and cliffs, of, for example, the Northern Corries and Braeriach. It can also be enhanced by the presence of wildlife.

2.   The sense of risk to life from exposure to the dangers of nature. This is the key feature of adventure in wild country and a major factor in the attraction of high-adventure sports such as mountaineering.

The Cairngorms, especially the high plateaux, provide strong elements of both kinds of wilderness. The areas above the tree line are the largest areas of ground holding largely natural vegetation in Britain and contain most of the indigenous animals and birds. In the recreational sense, they are of outstanding wilderness quality, due to the extent of remote country and lack of human artifacts.

Although the areas immediately below the natural treeline have been almost entirely deforested, in a peculiar sense the bleakness and openness of the resulting landscape increases the sense of exposure to nature and the elements, and enhances the wilderness experience, as it does in much of the Scottish Highlands. These open areas contain a considerable element of risk for the unwary and unskilled venturing among them, due to the unpredictable, dangerous climate, the considerable navigational problems in the frequent mists or snowstorms, the relative remoteness of much of the area, and the seriousness of the climbing in the corries around them.

More than any other British range, the Cairngorms can provide a 'total' mountain experience. I would therefore rate the wilderness value of the Cairngorms above that of any other British mountain range and above that of all but a few other areas in the EC countries. This, combined with their characteristics of providing a wide range of recreational opportunity and their diversity, give them a recreational value at local, national, and international levels.

The diversity and scale of the Cairngorms have produced a distinct approach to these mountains among the climbers and hillmen of north-east Scotland where the traditional bond with the Cairngorms is longest and deepest. The effects of these long approaches through the foothills and the experience of the wild high tops on every climbing day in the Cairngorms are profound. There are no quick climbs from the road as in Glencoe. Each climb is an expedition, a *complete mountain day*. Each involves in part at least a wilderness experience. In addition, most regular users of the area participate in a range of pursuits such as rock climbing, hill walking, and ski touring, plus some incidental bird watching and botanising.

All this has produced in local climbers in north-east Scotland a more holistic approach to their mountains and their mountaineering than climbers in most other areas of the world. The classic north-east climber and hillwalker is concerned with the experience of the whole mountain, of the whole day, and all that is seen and experienced throughout it, including the wildlife and landscape, not just the tussle with that day's rock or hill ascent.

THE DEGRADATION OF THE CAIRNGORMS

Notwithstanding all that the Cairngorms have to offer, for over two hundred years their natural and recreational resources have been progressively degraded. This problem has been well documented elsewhere (Curry-Lindahl *et al.* 1982; Watson 1988, this book). A brief summary of the trends is all that is necessary to demonstrate the scale and sadness of what is happening.

Large areas of the remaining Old Caledonian pine forest were felled in both world wars, though following the first world war some seed trees were left to replace the forest by regeneration. Afterwards the losses were by attrition including death of seedling trees caused by muirburning and more so by deer grazing, rather than large-scale clear felling. By 1987, a survey by the Royal Society for the Protection of Birds (RSPB) showed that another thirty per cent of the ancient pine forests had disappeared since 1957 (Bain 1987). The remnants were becoming remnants of remnants. With a few exceptions, even those were in poor shape, populated by ageing trees and with few young trees to replace them. The ancient pines where we first wandered in Glen Quoich thirty years ago are still there, but they are fewer and more ancient, and little real progress has been made to resolving the regeneration problem.

The Nature Conservancy Council (NCC) is arranging management agreements under which areas are fenced off to allow regeneration of the young trees (Matthew this book) but this is an entirely inadequate measure. The main reason for the continuing decline of the old forests is overgrazing by excessive numbers of red deer. When we crossed the Dee on that first day so long ago there were already too many deer in the Cairngorms to permit this regeneration. The spectacle of the deer at least is still available to newcomers to the Cairngorms, and more, for there are increasing numbers of red deer, and the feeble attempts of the Red Deer Commission to have them reduced remain ineffective (Red Deer Commission 1988). In 1967, according to the Commission's figures, there were about 23 700 red deer in the Cairngorms, and by 1983 some 34 000. Numbers have increased considerably since then.

Muirburn and overgrazing have caused great diminution of that other beautiful forest inhabitant, the birch, and many of the remaining fragments of birchwood are also dying.

The use of fire to prevent the growth of trees and to encourage the regrowth of heather which becomes less nutritious as a source of browse as it gets older, is an old one. It has been practised extensively on the heather moors and hills of the Cairngorms for a long time to maintain open areas for deer and grouse. This has been a major cause of the failure of the forests to regenerate. Frequently, quite substantial areas of young trees are burned deliberately, and even those too big to be destroyed that way may be cut down. Often too, the general management of the muirburn has been and remains bad. Too large areas are burned at one time, or areas are burned when the heather has been allowed to grow rank, causing hot fires that kill plant seeds in the top layers of soil. These areas then fail to 'green over' rapidly and the bare soil can then erode. Fires are often allowed to burn uphill into soil types that cannot withstand the impact, and on occasion even into standing forest. Well-practised muirburn is in fact the exception rather than the rule.

The most striking extensive intrusion into the central Cairngorms has undoubtedly been bulldozed tracks for easier access by deer hunters and grouse shooters. This began in the late 1950s, and by 1981 a survey showed that over 560 kilometres of new bulldozed tracks had appeared in Grampian Region, and a further 103 kilometres had obliterated old footpaths (Watson 1984). Most of the tracks are within the Cairngorms, and further damage of this kind has occurred within that part of the Cairngorms lying inside Highland Region and not included in the Grampian survey.

The results were disastrous. The area of wild remote country, distant from any road, shrank to a small fraction of its former size (Watson 1984, this book). Today, if a young person new to the Cairngorms repeated our early adventure up Glen Quoich to Beinn a' Bhuird, he or she would find not a footpath and unscarred landscape, but an ugly bulldozed track rising to 1100 metres on the shoulder of the mountain. Well loved landscapes were badly scarred, such as that crossing the view from Lochnagar. This scarring was increased by most of the tracks being badly made, so that they eroded in heavy rain, and the soil and rubble deposited downhill extended the scars.

Many tracks extended to the upper gentler slopes, where vehicles were then driven for long distances in any direction without a track. These have been used by scrambling motorbicycles and tourist four-wheel drive vehicles to gain access to plateaux. Vehicles used in this sensitive terrain cause extensive and enduring damage to soils and vegetation, quite apart from their intrusion on the wilderness experience in wild places.

It is difficult to see any adequate justification of this damage. The reason often given is that the venison of deer shot on the hill must reach a cold store within a short period stipulated under EEC regulations if it is to be exported to Europe, but most of the tracks were built before such regulations were introduced. The truth is that the type of customers for shooting deer and grouse changed. They were no longer willing to walk the distances that their predecessors did, and the convenience of the wealthy few prevailed over the interests of the non-wealthy many. It is an old story in the Cairngorms.

A major feature of the high Cairngorms is their sensitivity to overuse. Vegetation holds the soil in place, but at high altitudes the growing season is short and cool, and the soils of most of the Cairngorms are thin, gritty and infertile. Thus, when the vegetation is damaged by trampling, it takes a long time to recover, and repeated damage leads to the baring of soil that can then be eroded by wind and rain. Such environmentally sensitive areas are easily damaged by treading and can withstand only low levels of human use. Formerly, the very remoteness of the upper areas protected them from such overuse, but the building of a public road to Coire Cas, and the subsequent opening up of the chairlift in summer to near the summit of Cairn Gorm brought mass access to the very centre of what was once the remote heartland of the wild Cairngorms, and right to the very boundary of the high plateaux and the most valuable and sensitive part of the Cairngorms National Nature Reserve. The resulting spread of footpaths and associated erosion, of litter and numerous other problems within the reserve has again been well described (Watson this book).

THE INADEQUACY OF MEASURES FOR THE CONSERVATION OF THE CAIRNGORMS

The picture that can be seen to emerge from the above examples is one of the degradation of possibly the most valuable natural and recreational resource in Britain. It has not been a sudden thing that people would have recognised as wrong immediately. The story of the Cairngorms is the story of a slow disaster, insidious because the very gradualness, scale and complexity of the event made it difficult for many to perceive what was happening. Time and again in the Cairngorms a choice has had to be made between the private short term interest of landowners or others, and the broad long term public interest, and time and again it is the public interest that has taken second place. Yet if you get out a map and draw out the boundaries of nature reserves, scenic areas, and so on, much of the area is covered in protective designations. They are almost uniformly ineffective (see Curry-Lindahl this book).

The Cairngorms National Nature Reserve was declared in 1954, chiefly to protect the shrinking remnants of the Old Caledonian pine forest. Neither this, nor the associated designation of Sites of Special Scientific Interest (SSSI) have prevented overgrazing by red deer continuing to destroy the forest, or even the development of forest plantations, often of exotic conifers, within or near the forest remnants. Nor did it prevent the use of the Coire Cas chairlift on Cairn Gorm in summer to deposit up to 1000 people a day on to the summit of the mountain, giving easy mass access right to the boundary of the Natural Nature Reserve and to the sensitive tundra of the plateau.

Attempts by legislation to give the wildlife, landscape and wild country of the Cairngorms the protection they merit have been a mixture of the farcically ineffective when introduced, or potentially disastrous had they been introduced. It is worthwhile to recount the main events.

In 1947, the Ramsay Committee recommended that the Cairngorms along with four other areas in the Scottish Highlands be designated a National Park (HMSO 1947). The proposals of the Ramsay Committee were considerably more radical than those for England and Wales. They owed more to the American example of National Parks, proposing that land within National Parks should be acquired by the nation either voluntarily or compulsorily. Perhaps the very radicalism of the proposals were their undoing, for they are thought to have foundered on the resistance of the landed interests and others. It is generally thought that the failure to do so was entirely damaging for the future of the Cairngorms, but this is probably not the case. Nowadays, it is increasingly recognised that the great need is to increase the protection of such an area from too great ease of access and pressures for development. The approach of the Ramsay Committee was quite strongly developmental, encompassing various ideas for development within National Parks. The construction of roads, long-distance footpaths etc., were all part of what they envisaged.

This 'developmental approach' to protected areas was carried much further in an attempt to produce an overall strategy for the Cairngorms area in 1967. A report called *Cairngorm Area* was produced by a group from the Scottish Development Department and local planning authorities concerned (Scottish Development Department 1967). It proposed that to help meet 'the nation's increasing needs for outdoor recreation of all kinds', new roads should be built through Glen Feshie and Glen Tilt, to Beinn a' Bhuird, between Nethy Bridge and Glen More, and between Tomintoul and Crathie in Deeside, and to Coire na Ciste and Lurcher's Gully. Downhill skiing developments were planned for Beinn a' Bhuird. Only three out of the report's seventy-eight pages were concerned with conservation of the area. It would have been a disastrous plan, carving the Cairngorms up into isolated units and giving much easier access to the most remote areas.

A later attempt by the Countryside Commission for Scotland to have areas such as the Cairngorms designated as Special Parks (Countryside Commission for Scotland 1974) was turned down by the Secretary of State for Scotland. Since Special Parks were really a model based on the English and Welsh National Parks, the implementation of this proposal would also have been unfortunate. For example it placed the protection of nationally-important resources in the hands of local politicians.

When the recommendations of the Ramsay Committee were turned down, five National Park Direction Areas (NPDA), essentially the areas examined by the Committee, including the Cairngorms, were designated under the Town & Country Planning (General Development) (Scotland) Order of 1948. County Councils, as they were then, were required to furnish the Secretary of State for Scotland with details of all development proposals within those areas. As a protective measure they ignored such land uses as afforestation, deer shooting and agriculture, and were negative and pro-active in their approach. They were largely ineffective.

In 1980, they were abolished and replaced by forty National Scenic Areas (NSAs), including the large Cairngorms NSA. Within these, any development given planning permission by a local authority but objected to by the Countryside Commission for Scotland, had to be referred to the Secretary of State for Scotland. The legal requirement for planning permission was also extended to certain developments including all buildings over twelve metres high, including buildings for agriculture and forestry, and all bulldozed tracks above 300 metres altitude. Their performance in dealing with one major problem, bulldozed tracks, is a measure of their lack of success. Most bulldozed tracks for example are below 300 metres. The requirement regarding bulldozed tracks was extended down to sea level in 1987 when the great majority of the tracks that were likely to be built had already been bulldozed. Since then, two landowners within the Cairngorms have bulldozed tracks or parts of tracks without planning permission. Both have received 'retrospective planning permission'. As shown here and proved clearly by recent research (Cobham Research Consultants 1988; Land Use Consultants 1989) NSAs have been almost completely ineffective.

If the Cairngorms have retained much of their original value for wildlife and recreation, then it is not because of the protective designations put upon them. Much of what appears to be conservation in the Cairngorms is really simply the result of luck and benign neglect.

THE FUTURE OF THE CAIRNGORMS

What must be done to protect this marvellous range of mountains for the benefit both of Scotland and of the wildlife of the Cairngorms? We must have vision, and determination. We must have a vision of what the Cairngorms could be like within our own lifetime and in a hundred years, and be determined to fight for it. Above all, the many thousands of people who have taken from the Cairngorms by enjoying them, being challenged by them, and finding renewal in them, must put something back into them.

What should our vision be? One feature of the Cairngorms that we have never fully explored is their potential. The relative infertility of their soils has meant that they have been little colonised or developed. As a result, they contain no settlements within or close to their main massifs, except in Glen More. They thus have an enormous potential for the 'development' of truly wild country, with the natural regeneration of much of the natural forest and scrub cover of the Highlands plus its associated wildlife. This proposal is not part of some plan to return the whole of the Scottish Highlands to this state, but wild country is a shrinking resource all over the world just at a time when the world is discovering an increasing need for it, and there are certain parts of the Highlands well suited to this use.

Whatever the vision we pursue, there is a need for mountaineers, hill walkers and other hill users to decide how it should be achieved. There are only two choices. We can buy them or lobby politically for a better form of legal protection which might include purchase by the state. Either way, mountaineers, hill walkers and others have ample opportunity to 'put something back' into the Cairngorms by lending their support. If it is decided that the way forward is for better protective legislation, then this will require some hard work pressing for the right measures.

Whatever the measures, they will have to meet certain basic requirements of management which my co-authors and I tried to outline in our booklet *The Future of the Cairngorms.* These are:

1. There must be a national management plan for the Cairngorms to bring unified management to the area.

2. Protection of the Cairngorms must be increased to internationally agreed standards under this plan.

3. National priorities should take priority over local ones within this plan.

4. Planning policy must recognise that wild areas are a shrinking resource subject to increasing use.

5. The prime land uses of different parts of the area should be defined and protected.

6. The recreational users of the area should be consulted on the management of the area.

7. Renewed natural landscapes should be encouraged.

8. Tourist developments must be in balance with what the area can withstand.

These eight management goals were the product of much thought and experience, and after seven years they still seem to me to be the minimum standard to achieve.

REFERENCES

BAIN, C. (1987). *Native Pinewoods in Scotland – A Review 1957-1987.* Royal Society for the Protection of Birds, Edinburgh.

COBHAM RESOURCE CONSULTANTS (1988). *The Effectiveness of Landscape Designation in Scotland.* Cobham Resource Consultants, Edinburgh.

COUNTRYSIDE COMMISSION FOR SCOTLAND (1974). *A Park System for Scotland.* Countryside Commission for Scotland, Perth.

CURRY-LINDAHL, K. (1974). *Survey of Northern and Western European National Parks and Equivalent Reserves.* United Nations Environment Programme, Nairobi.

107

CURRY-LINDAHL, K., WATSON, A. & WATSON, R.D. (1982). *The Future of the Cairngorms.* North East Mountain Trust, Aberdeen.

HMSO (1947). *National Parks and the Conservation of Nature (Scotland).* Command Paper 7235, HMSO, London.

LAND USE CONSULTANTS (1989). *National Scenic Areas – A Review of the Pilot Studies Loch Rannoch and Glen Lyon National Scenic Area and Eildon and Leaderfoot National Scenic Area.* Land Use Consultants, Edinburgh.

MURRAY, W.H. (1989). *Save the Cairngorms Campaign Bulletin No. 2.* Save the Cairngorms Campaign, Inverness.

RED DEER COMMISSION (1988). *Annual Report for 1987.* HMSO, Edinburgh.

SCOTTISH DEVELOPMENT DEPARTMENT (1967). *Cairngorms Area.* HMSO, Edinburgh.

STEVEN, H.M. & CARLISLE, A. (1959). *The Native Pinewoods of Scotland.* Oliver & Boyd, Edinburgh & London.

WATSON, A. (1984). A survey of vehicular hill tracks in north-east Scotland for land use planning. *Journal of Environmental Management,* **18**, 345-353.

WATSON, A. (1988). Decline of the wild. *Cairngorms at the Crossroads* (ed by J. Crumley), pp 8-13. Scottish Wild Land Group, Edinburgh.

THE CAIRNGORMS NATIONAL NATURE RESERVE (NNR), THE FOREMOST BRITISH CONSERVATION AREA OF INTERNATIONAL SIGNIFICANCE

KAI CURRY-LINDAHL

Grenstigen 3, 18133 Lidingo, Stockholm, Sweden

INTRODUCTION

The Cairngorms National Nature Reserve (NNR) was established in 1954 and increased in area in 1966 (Matthew this book). In 1977, the Nature Conservancy Council (NCC) declared in a draft to a Statement of Policies, included in the second revision of a *Management Plan for 1977-1981,* that

> management and recreational use of the land in the period 1960-1975 have not been in the best interests of nature conservation. A more constructive attitude to the conservation of this Reserve is needed urgently if the Cairngorms are to continue as one of Britain's finest wildlife and landscape areas.

The First Management Plan (1959) gave the reasons for the establishment and the contemporary values of the Cairngorms NNR as follows:

> ... for the purpose of conserving its native woodlands and mountain habitats with their characteristic plants and animals, so that these may persist and develop naturally with a minimum of interference from man's activities but nevertheless subject to scientific management based on observation, éxperience and experiment (Nature Conservancy 1959).

It was also emphasized at the time of the declaration that the Reserve provided unique opportunities for studying the ecology of mountain birds, plants and insects, high altitude meteorology, and research on the natural regeneration of native Scots pine from the remnants of the Old Caledonian forest.

In the same management plan the two main objectives of the Cairngorms NNR were defined:

> *Perpetuation objective.* To protect the biological and physical features of the Reserve and to allow their natural evolution with a minimum of interference from man's activities
> *and*
> *Appreciation objective.* To encourage the appreciation and study of the Reserve for activities which are dependent on its special natural qualities, providing this is compatible with the first objective.

These objectives and management plans, stated by the Nature Conservancy set the stage in clear terms for Great Britain's foremost conservation area. It is tragic that they have not been followed.

As came out so bluntly at the Public Inquiry in 1981 concerning the proposed downhill skiing development into Lurcher's Gully, the Cairngorms NNR is rapidly deteriorating due to pressure from different kinds of land use which are antagonistic to the aims of the Reserve (Scottish Development Department 1982; Scottish Affairs Committee 1985).

The result of the 1981 Lurcher's Gully Public Inquiry was perceived by many as a victory for conservation. Its verdict, broadly upheld by the then Secretary of State for Scotland, favoured the views presented by the conservation/recreation side. I interpreted the Inquiry in Kingussie as a part of the democratic process. Therefore, for me as a foreigner, it is difficult to understand why in 1986 a new Secretary of State, of the same political party as in 1981, allowed the erection of snow fencing in the Northern Corries. On what grounds? As far as I know there are no new elements, other than the fact that the conservation arguments of today are even stronger than in 1981.

This political tragi-comedy is not only a democratic and judicial failure, but also, it seems to me, another demonstration of how the NCC neglects to defend the prime British NNR.

During all the conflicts over the Cairngorms NNR since the 1970s, the NCC has, in my view, been astonishingly passive. In so far as the Cairngorms are concerned, the NCC either is a paper tiger or its senior management for the past fifteen years has not been conservation-minded about the Cairngorms.

The NCC has never fully utilized the tools given to it by its constitution, in particular its statutory powers of compulsory purchase. If the process of acquiring land for NNRs and/or of reaching ecologically appropriate agreements with landowners is so slow that valuable areas, which ought to be set aside as fully controlled NNRs, face irreversible alterations, then compulsory acquisition should occur.

In order not to be misunderstood, I repeat what I already said in 1974 in a report to the International Union for the Conservation of Nature and Natural Resources (IUCN) and the NCC on Great Britain:

> the NCC has wisely avoided utilizing its power of compulsory land acquisition which has certainly facilitated many existing NNR agreements with landowners (Curry-Lindahl 1974).

However, there are situations when the ultimate line of defence has to be put in action. I feel strongly that, as regards the Cairngorms, after twenty years of devastation this moment has now come.

CHARACTERISTICS OF THE CAIRNGORMS IN AN INTERNATIONAL CONTEXT

The Cairngorms NNR is the largest and most spectacular nature reserve in Great Britain. It is also the most genuine natural area of the British Isles. The montane habitats with their vegetation and wild animals are a living heritage of past Britain from post-glacial time through the millenia until today.

Internationally it is of significance and importance primarily to Europe as an example of arctic-alpine environments in a relatively southern latitude. But the Cairngorms also represent other types of valuable assets which contribute to the Reserve's position as the foremost conservation area of the UK, for example:

as a mountain range, as the largest area of ground over 900 metres;

as wilderness country;

as the most important area for montane wildlife in the countries of the European Community (EC);

as the most arctic-like terrain with a wide range of landforms in Europe south of Iceland and Scandinavia;

as the largest tract of land least modified by man in Britain;

as the most natural and varied landscape in Scotland;

as the most diverse moorland in Britain;

and

as the largest expanses of Old Caledonian pine forest in the British Isles.

Yet, despite all these scientific, scenic, educational and recreational qualifications the Cairngorms are repeatedly mismanaged, mistreated and under constant threat of being even more damaged.

As to scenic values, the Scottish Tourist Board admits that the beauty of unspoiled scenery in Scotland attracts more people than any other factor. It is:

> 'the country's greatest asset; it is also the asset that can be so easily and irretrievably lost' (Scottish Tourist Board 1969).

THE DECLINE OF THE CAIRNGORMS

The fact that the Reserve was established for the specific purpose of conserving its native woodlands and mountain habitats etc, makes the devastation in the area over the last twenty years almost incredible.

Recently Watson (1988) published a catalogue of the changes that have seriously reduced the wild qualities of the Cairngorms. Most of these alterations to the wilderness area have occurred since 1950. Morris (1976) pointed out the increasing erosion due to human pressure in the 1960s and 1970s. The damage was particularly severe to arctic-alpine heaths and turf. In a more detailed paper on soil erosion and vegetation damage, Watson (1985) showed that severe damage is also extending well inside the Cairngorms NNR.

In 1974, I was commissioned by IUCN and the NCC to assess the international standing of Britain's National Nature Reserves and National Parks. Already at that time I ranked the Cairngorms as Britain's foremost conservation area, but also described how even then they were being damaged and gravely threatened by unwise developments (Curry-Lindahl 1974).

I have visited the Cairngorms on later occasions and each time I feel that all the new evidence points to the fact that my 1974 recommendations are more necessary now than they were earlier.

As my report to IUCN (Curry-Lindahl 1974) (and through this organization to the NCC) on Great Britain has never been published in the U.K. (although cited here and there) I quote some passages on the Cairngorms:

> Despite being the largest wilderness area of Great Britain the Cairngorms NNR is not free from problems due to the pattern of ownership. This is the root to all problems that the reserve is facing. The area is only to a minor part owned by the NCC. For the other parts exist agreements with private land owners, but they have much to say and each of them run their areas according to their own interests. This is, of course, legitimate, but not always in the long-term interest of conservation.

In fact, the environmental problems that press upon the Cairngorms NNR are manifold and may turn out to be fatal for the long-term conservation and evolution of the Reserve to a natural state, which should be one of its aims.

Among several adverse man-made factors, the following seem to be most important for the future of the Cairngorms NNR:

a. overbrowsing by excessive numbers of red deer (due to overstocking) which leads to suppression of the pine forest and a lowering of the timber line;

b. the management of the red deer seems to be too much influenced by the landowners' hunting interests;

c. the provision of artificial supplementary food for wintering red deer in certain areas obstructs a natural regulation of the population in relation to the carrying capacity of the Reserve;

d.   the fencing by the Forestry Commission along the western boundary of the Reserve has cut off important migration routes and winter feeding areas of the red deer, which causes an increased grazing pressure in certain areas inside the Reserve;

e.   the opening up of the Reserve through the construction of roads in order to facilitate shooting is not desirable from a general conservation point of view and has led to increased public pressure on high ground as a result of using these roads for automobiles, motor bicycles, pedal cycles and access on foot;

f.   is the burning of heaths really necessary inside the Reserve for reasons other than to prevent fires from outside?

g.   the impact of tourism, particularly in the northern part of the Reserve;

h.   the tendency (so far only suggestions) to give up areas on the periphery of the Reserve due to pressure from increased activities of tourism;

i.   the water pipeline to Aviemore and the great scars it caused inside the Reserve;

j.   dogs running free inside the Reserve;

k.   the accumulation of litter at certain sites during the winter;

l.   the introduction of an apparently unsuitable stock of reindeer to the area.

Continual development schemes are nibbling more and more of the natural history assets of the Reserve, both directly and indirectly, through destruction of the immediate surroundings of the Reserve.

THE INTERNATIONAL SIGNIFICANCE
OF THE CAIRNGORMS

The international significance of the Cairngorms has been testified on numerous occasions at international meetings and assemblies on various continents, as well as by international conventions and treaties. These include:

1971. Convention on Wetlands of International Importance, especially as Waterfowl Habitat. The lochs of the Cairngorms are listed. Adopted in Ramsar, Iran; in force 1975.

1980. The World Conservation Strategy of the United Nations Environment Programme (UNEP) and IUCN recognized the importance of the Scottish Highlands and recommended that priority to secure protection of both mountain and highland systems should be established (IUCN 1980a).

1981. IUCN General Assembly, meeting in Christchurch, New Zealand, passed a resolution calling on the British Government to:

> take all practical steps to secure for the Cairngorm Mountains protection appropriate to their international significance.

1982. In *The World's Greatest Natural Areas* IUCN issued an Indicative Inventory of Natural Sites of World Heritage Quality, being selected as candidates for inclusion in the World Cultural and Natural Heritage Convention. Adopted at UNESCO in Paris in 1975. In force since 1975. Only two sites in the UK were recognized, the Cairngorms and St Kilda (IUCN 1982).

1983. Third World Wilderness Congress, meeting in Scotland, passed a resolution strongly recommending that the UK Government:

> urgently consider the creation of World Heritage Sites in the Scottish Highlands and gives priority to such a site in the Cairngorms Area to protect the full range of mountain, forest, and wetland environments.

1987. Fourth World Wilderness Congress, meeting in Colorado, expressed its deep concern that no progress has been made towards establishing the Cairngorms Area as a World Heritage Site and notes that this area is not included in the official tentative list which the British Government intends to nominate to the World Heritage List in the next five to ten years. The Congress urged:

> the British Government to take all practical steps to secure for the Cairngorms Area protection appropriate to its international significance and to nominate this area for inscription on the World Heritage List.

These statements on the importance of the Cairngorms for conservation reflect the widely accepted view that the area is of exceptional value not only to Britain but also to Europe and to the world community as a global asset.

Therefore, it appears as an absurd paradox that neither the British Government nor the NCC have tried to remedy the situation by acquiring the whole area as a strict nature reserve. It is now high time to do so before the Cairngorms become irreversibly destroyed.

WHY IS GREAT BRITAIN SO SLOW ON CONSERVATION?

It is tragic that Great Britain's largest, most spectacular and biologically most important National Nature Reserve – the Cairngorms and adjacent

Sites of Special Scientific Interest (SSSI), are not under the aegis of one agency. Instead, they are run and managed by six central government bodies, two Regional Councils, three District Councils, several private landowners, a development board, and a chairlift company. In fact, the NCC owns only twelve per cent of the Cairngorms NNR.

In view of the outstanding natural history values and the recognized international significance of the Cairngorms, particularly in the European context, it is an anomaly that the Government through the NCC is not in practice responsible for the management of the entire area.

How is it possible that such an advanced and modern country as Great Britain seems to lack elementary legislation for the safeguarding of its most valuable conservation area? Or has the UK not the political will or courage to apply the existing legislation?

It is a shame that during the past twenty years Great Britain has not made an effort to protect adequately its foremost natural area. I am sure that future generations of Britons will find this governmental neglect inexcusable.

Whatever the explanation to the present situation of governmental passivity in relation to the Cairngorms, it is extraordinary. Was not the UK the first state in post-war Europe to establish a conservation organization based on ecological criteria – the Nature Conservancy? Moreover, Great Britain participated wholeheartedly from the beginning in the international conservation field. In fact, it was much more advanced in conservation in its former colonies than at home.

Therefore, the Government's and the NCC's present indifference to the future of the Cairngorms is hard to understand. The management policy for this reserve seems to be dictated by the diverse interests of landowners, concessionary companies and the Highlands and Islands Development Board (HIDB). In this hotch-potch of conflicting intentions and aims, the conservation considerations are firmly represented only by NCC's twelve per cent ownership. This means that it is farcical to claim that the NCC is responsible for the management of the Cairngorms NNR. In this administrative chaos, a coordinated, long-term land use and management plan is entirely lacking. In this scramble-supper of exploiters, the voice of the NCC is hardly audible. Thus the conservation points of view in the management of the Reserve are lost amongst a chorus of other interests. The latter are advocating land use practices which too often are adverse to conservation and the principles for which a NNR should stand.

Though I understand the NCC's hesitation to use its power of land acquisition, I feel that the application of this instrument is justifiable to apply in the interest of the nation and future generations of people when the objective is to save the country's prime conservation area.

RECOMMENDATIONS FOR THE CAIRNGORMS

It is regrettable that in 1988 the recommendations which I suggest for the Cairngorms are those that I put forward in 1974. Fourteen years have been lost, and today the situation is worse.

Since the Cairngorms NNR is the foremost conservation area of Great Britain, an effort should be made to speed up the process of acquiring land within the reserve to correspond to an area of such conservation importance.

1.   The Glen More Forest Park should be incorporated into the NNR and the exotic species of trees unwisely introduced should be removed.

2.   The Forestry Commission should be advised that its policy in areas adjacent to the NNR must always give priority to the purpose and best interests of this Reserve. Therefore, the fence along the western boundary ought to be removed.

3.   A clear conservation policy with long-term perspectives must be established as guidelines for land use planning and resource management of all public and private bodies involved. It is up to the Government to show a constructive leadership in this field.

4.   Reduction of the red deer population to a level where natural regeneration of the native Caledonian Forest occurs.

5.   Ban on artificial feeding of red deer.

6.   Elimination of the present stock of reindeer inside the Reserve. The present herd, introduced from Swedish Lapland, is a domesticated forest form, not the domesticated mountain or wild form. The herd apparently cannot exist in the wild and has been given supplementary artificial food for many years. To say that this herd is well-established in the Cairngorms (Southern 1964) seems to be an ironical overstatement.

7.   Within the Reserve, the NCC can veto the building of roads and pipelines. It also has the control over any water regulations which affect the reserve.

8.   No area whatsoever of the NNR should be given up because outside pressures are high. A retreat of the boundary will lead only to progressively increased pressure in other areas of the Reserve.

9.   Due to thin snow cover, the vegetation is often damaged. Skiing activities and developments inside the NNR and SSSI should therefore be carefully monitored.

10. Several signboards at various strategic sites on the NNR boundary at the Cairngorms plateau and close to the ski lifts should inform visitors that they are approaching the NNR and will soon have a fine outlook over the most important nature reserve in Great Britain.

11. To stop dogs running free in British NNRs requires a change of legislation; this should be done, allowing only owners whose dogs are on the lead or at heel, access. In other European countries, no dogs run free between April 1 and October 1, and they are banned from nature reserves.

ZONING

For the Cairngorms NNR, consideration should be given to introduce a system of zoning as defined by IUCN on pages 23-31 in the 1974 United Nations List of National Parks and Equivalent Reserves (IUCN 1974).

This would reduce the vulnerability of the Cairngorms to influences from human activities in surrounding areas. The Cairngorms NNR is heavily subjected to inappropriate landuse practices and tourist industry development right up to the boundary of the NNR.

Hence zoning should be established as soon as possible for the Cairngorms.

A COMPARISON OF NATURE RESERVES AND NATIONAL PARKS IN BRITAIN AND EUROPE

Before dealing with national parks and nature reserves in Great Britain it is necessary to point out that the British terminology for such areas differs widely from that adopted by almost all other nations of the world. Some of the NNRs, the highest category of nature reserves in the UK, correspond to what the Council of Europe defines as Categories A and B. By contrast, the National Parks of Great Britain, according to the Council of Europe, are put in Category C. To me British National Parks seem, in general, to correspond more to the Council of Europe's Category D, and in some cases do not justify even Category D (the lowest category), although parts of some National Parks are of high scientific value and merit adequate protection, which they presently do not have.

Higher categories of nature reserves have been defined and approved by the IUCN General Assembly 1969 and the Second World Conference on National Parks 1972* (IUCN 1974) – and the list given in Resolution (73) 30, 1973, by the Council of Europe for their Categories A and B as discussed in the above paragraph. None of the British reserves and National Parks qualify for any of these categories.

Since the Council of Europe's definitions and the comparative table included in the Resolution put the British NNRs in Categories A and B it should be stressed that Category A comprises:

> areas under complete protection where all human activities are prohibited,

while for areas in Category B:

> any artificial intervention which might modify their natural appearance, composition and evolution is prohibited.

Most NNRs in Britain are managed and that for very good reasons, but with a strict application to the Council of Europe's definitions, the British NNRs do not fall within the Council's Categories A and B.

In my opinion IUCN's definitions of various categories of nature reserves are more realistic than those of the Council of Europe. Their categories of protected areas were approved by the General Assembly 1972. In this there is a category of 'Protected Natural Zone' containing a sub-category of 'Managed Natural Zone'. The latter corresponds well with the situation in many British NNRs.

However, the best way of overcoming the classification difficulties of British NNRs would be to zone certain reserves. For example, in the Cairngorms NNR, various designated areas within the Reserve are entirely protected, some are managed, and others even cultivated. Zoning would enable the Cairngorms to be included in the highest categories of reserves in both the Council of Europe and IUCN.

In 1974, Britain's 135 NNRs covered nearly 121 500 hectares, with the Cairngorms NNR (25 950 hectares) the largest. In general, however, Britain's NNRs are numerous but small. There are thirty-six nature reserves in Europe that are larger than the Cairngorms. In the size category of 10 000-25 000 hectares, there are two in Great Britain and fifty in the remaining part of Europe. Although contributing largely to the ecological autonomy of certain areas, size alone is not always of the most significant importance.

*FOOTNOTE. These correspond to the United Nations concept of a national park or equivalent reserve, and are the basis for the United Nations List of National Parks and Equivalent Reserves.

The rules for visitors in nature reserves seem to be more restricted in most other countries of Europe than in many UK reserves. Landownership in many British nature reserves differs widely from most of those in Europe, although there are similarities with some countries. Leases or temporary agreements with landowners are not the best solution for the long-term management of a nature reserve.

When comparisons are made between British NNRs and non-European nature reserves of higher categories, the differences appear even more striking. This is again chiefly due to the different ownership of land and different historic traditions of legislation in Great Britain.

For the long-term existence and management of the larger and most important NNRs it would be advantageous if they could be taken over entirely as soon as possible by a single authority such as the NCC, in such a way that this agency is not hampered in its management efforts by antagonistic measures applied in and around the NNR.

Such a step is certainly desirable for the Cairngorms NNR. But it is also necessary to take efficient measures to protect and conserve a larger area – the whole 3885 square kilometres of the Cairngorms Area – from being severely damaged by further unnecessary developments.

This could be achieved either through an enlargement of the Cairngorms NNR or in the form of a World Heritage Site including both the NNR and the surrounding area.

Such a conservation scheme for the Cairngorms is hardly the place for such a commercially operating development body as the HIDB, particularly after the strong disapproval of its ski development projects by the Public Inquiry of 1981 (Scottish Development Department 1982) and later by a Parliamentary Select Committee (Scottish Affairs Committee 1985).

In 1987 it was suggested by the Countryside Commission for Scotland that the 3885 square kilometres of the Cairngorms Area should be set aside as a national park. This is, of course, better than no protection at all, but from what I have seen of the British style of national parks I believe it would be safer for the Cairngorms to be fully protected by a NNR, controlled and managed by the NCC only.

By international standards the Cairngorms are poorly protected whatever the statutory background of the area, so it is high time to change this in a constructive way.

REFERENCES

CURRY-LINDAHL, K. (1974). *IUCN Survey of Northern and Western European National Parks and Equivalent Reserves.* Report on Great Britain, pp.1-20. United Nations Environment programme, Nairobi.

IUCN (1974). *Second World Conference on National Parks* (ed. by Sir Hugh Elliot). IUCN Publications New Series No. 29, 1-78, Lucerne, Switzerland.

IUCN (1980). *World Conservation Strategy.* IUCN, Gland, Switzerland.

IUCN (1982). *The World's Greatest Natural Areas.* IUCN, Gland, Switzerland.

MORRIS, D. (1976). The promotion of the conservation of mountain areas. *Conserving the Mountains.* 15pp. British Mountaineering Council, Manchester.

NATURE CONSERVANCY (1959). *Cairngorms National Nature Reserve. Management Plan.* Nature Conservancy, Edinburgh.

SCOTTISH AFFAIRS COMMITTEE (1985). *Second Report Session 1984-85, Highlands and Islands Development Board.* HMSO, London.

SCOTTISH DEVELOPMENT DEPARTMENT (1982). *Findings of the Lurcher's Gully Public Inquiry, Kingussie.* Scottish Development Department, Edinburgh.

SCOTTISH TOURIST BOARD (1969). *Caravanning and Camping in Scotland.* Selected Studies No.8.

SOUTHERN, H.N. (1964). *The Handbook of British Mammals.* Blackwell, Oxford.

WATSON, A. (1985). Soil erosion and vegetation damage near ski lifts at Cairn Gorm, Scotland. *Biological Conservation,* **33**, 363-381.

WATSON, A. (1988). Decline of the wild. *Cairngorms at the Crossroads* (ed. by J. Crumley), pp. 8-13. Scottish Wild Land Group, Edinburgh.

EAST CAIRNGORMS MANAGEMENT PLAN – PROJECT OUTLINE

GRAMPIAN REGIONAL COUNCIL, DEPARTMENT OF PHYSICAL PLANNING,
Woodhill House, Westburn Road, Aberdeen AB9 2LU

SUMMARY

1. Additional recreational and economic demands are being made on the Cairngorms at a time when the area's natural assets are being increasingly recognised for their national and international importance. Traditional town and country planning cannot alone address the problems and conflicts which result. Grampian Regional Council is working towards the adoption of a Management Plan for the East Cairngorms, bounded by the Cairngorms watershed to the north-west, the River Dee to the south and the A939 road to the north-east.

2. The objectives embrace conservation, social and economic benefit and access for recreation. The aim is to establish an agreed framework within which competing activites can be reconciled, and a basis for a coordinated programme of action.

3. A Core Group, drawn from Regional and District Councils, the Countryside Commission for Scotland, the Nature Conservancy Council, the Scottish Landowners Federation and the Scottish Wildlife and Countryside Link, is preparing an Issues Report which will be the subject of public consultation.

4. Following this, and depending on the response, the Core Group will be expanded to become a Steering Group with the task of preparing the Management Plan in draft. This will embrace administration, conservation priorities, resource management, development opportunities, planning strategy and controls, and procedures for monitoring and review. It is hoped that, in final form, the East Cairngorms Management Plan will not only be approved by the relevant statutory bodies but also be accepted by, and incorporated in the work of, a wide variety of private and voluntary bodies.

INTRODUCTION

National and international attention is increasingly being focused on conservation of the Cairngorms as it becomes clearer that the area has natural properties which are, in global terms, in short supply. Likewise, the area's recreational and sporting potential is attracting an increasing number of visitors into the mountains. Meantime, local people depend on the Cairngorms for their livelihood, whether directly through farming and forestry or indirectly through providing services to tourists.

These three aspects of the Cairngorms both co-exist and conflict with each other. For example, traditional land management practices support interesting wildlife and maintain the scenery which attracts many tourists. On the other hand, large-scale afforestation can sometimes be visually intrusive and environmentally damaging. The unexpected arrival of hillwalkers can disturb stalking.

Traditional town and country planning fails to address these problems, not least because many rural land uses are outwith planning control. This was recognised by Grampian Regional Council in the Rural Area Structure Plan (Grampian Regional Council 1984), which attempts to strike a balance between exploitation and conservation throughout Grampian. In practice, the requirement was for a widely-based approach which could accommodate the views and aspirations of the many and varied interests in the area.

The solution adopted was to propose the preparation of a Management Plan for the Cairngorms, in which all interested parties would liaise and contribute to an agreed approach to the otherwise intractable problems facing the area.

A project brief has been prepared by Grampian Regional Council, Department of Physical Planning for a Management Plan for the East Cairngorms, that part of the area within the administrative boundary of Grampian Region. The Plan will be advisory in nature, and the process of preparation will seek a commitment to implementing courses of action within an agreed framework.

This paper, which is based on the project brief, outlines the objectives of the Management Plan, identifies areas where relevant information is required, suggests a process within which the stages of analysis and plan preparation can be the subject of public consultation, and indicates a timescale within which the Plan can be prepared.

AREA

The initial area (Map 1) includes all the major summits of the Central Cairngorms massif – Cairn Toul, Braeriach, Ben Macdui, Cairn Gorm, Beinn a' Bhuird and Ben Avon – Loch Avon and Loch Etchachan, Glen Derry, Glen Dee, and Glen Avon. Also included are the villages of Braemar and Tomintoul, and the ski centre at the Lecht. The area covers 724 square kilometres.

The proposed boundary is based on:

a. the roads which give access to the area;

b. the Dee valley;

and

c. the Regional administrative boundary based on the Cairngorms watershed.

The area bears a strong resemblance to that proposed as a National Park by the Ramsay Committee (National Parks in Scotland) in 1947 (HMSO 1947). Excluded at present are Lochnagar with its adjacent National Scenic Area, Glen Clunie, the ski centre at Glenshee, and the village of Ballater. The area of the proposed Management Plan is flexible, and can be revised if necessary.

There are two areas, a *Proposals Area* and a *Context Area*. The *Proposals Area* is a tightly defined zone which encompasses the summits of the East Cairngorms and the associated principal sites of recreation. Management proposals will, in the first instance, be restricted to this area. Because of the relationship between this zone and the nearby settlements, however, a *Context Area* is proposed. This is larger and extends to just beyond the first ring of settlements.

The benefit of this two-tier designation is to allow the local population to make an appropriate contribution to the Plan so that the inter-relationship between the massif and the settlements can be planned for. It had been Grampian Regional Council's initial intention to have prepared a Management Plan for a much larger area of the Cairngorms, to include that part administered by Highland Regional Council. After initial discussions, however, Highland Regional Council felt it inappropriate to engage in such a joint study in advance of discussion of their revised Structure Plan, which is imminent. This does not discount the option of their becoming involved at a later date.

OBJECTIVES

The Management Plan objectives are, in order of precedence:

a. to conserve those natural attributes of the Cairngorms which are recognised as being of international, national or local importance. Those attributes include its landscape, flora and fauna;

b. subject to (a) above, to obtain the maximum sustainable social and economic benefit for the local communities in and adjoining the Cairngorms by all means possible, including recreation;

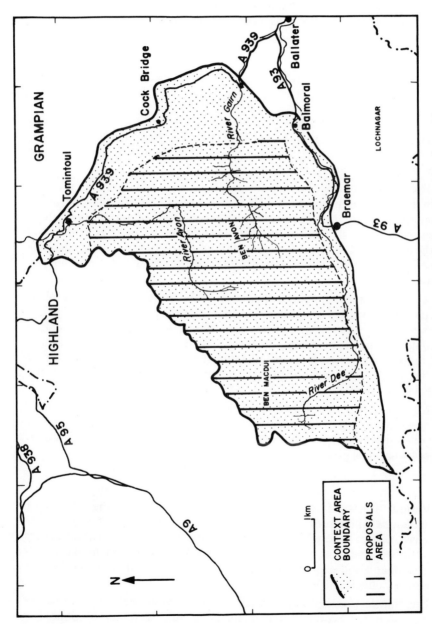

Map 1. The boundaries of the East Cairngorms Management Plan.

c. subject to (a) and (b) above, to obtain the maximum freedom of access for recreational users of the Cairngorms.

These objectives and their order of precedence were agreed by the Core Group (see Procedure section page 138) at its inaugural meeting in June 1988.

CONTEXT

A commitment to prepare a Management Plan for the Cairngorms was given in Grampian Regional Council's Rural Area Structure Plan which sets out the framework for development prepared by the Regional Council and approved by the Secretary of State.

The approved Structure Plan for the Rural Area of Grampian, together with Local Plans prepared by District Councils, will provide an initial framework for the Management Plan. Accordingly, all authorities will be required as a first step to identify existing and potential policies appropriate to the area. However, the Management Plan will be flexible so that changing situations and opportunities arising from reviews of these statutory Plans can be reflected in it.

A second starting point will therefore be other management plans prepared by a variety of agencies for their interests in the East Cairngorms. If necessary, the East Cairngorms Management Plan will contain recommendations for change in these and the statutory Plans. The co-operation and involvement of all interested parties, including statutory bodies, landowners and user groups, is essential and is being sought from the initial stages onwards.

All will have a role to play in formulating and implementing the East Cairngorms Management Plan, which, it is hoped, will help resolve some of the dilemmas posed by public access to the area and restrictions placed on them by national policy.

DESIGNATIONS

Various tracts of the East Cairngorms are already the subject of designations which seek to protect particular attributes. National Nature Reserve, Site of Special Scientific Interest and National Scenic Area are all statutory designations, whereas Site of Interest to Natural Science and Area of Regional Landscape Significance are established through Grampian Regional Council's Structure Plans.

The Nature Conservancy Council, in association with the Countryside Commission for Scotland, recommends to the Secretary of State for

Scotland the inclusion of the Cairngorms in the World Heritage List. This is supported by Grampian Regional Council. The Countryside Commission for Scotland has also suggested possible National Park designation, and there have also been suggestions that the area should be a Regional Park.

Together, existing designations already cover most of the Cairngorms (Maps 2a and 2b). Acceptance of the additional proposals would extend coverage throughout the proposals area of the Management Plan. If designations are to be successful in protecting the particular aspects of the natural environment to which they refer, and yet still permit economic and recreational use of the area, management of natural and human resources is required.

This Management Plan aims to establish:

a. an agreed framework within which competing activities can be reconciled;

b. a basis upon which a co-ordinated programme of action can be carried out.

THE KEY ISSUES

The most important single issue affecting the Cairngorms is the balance to be achieved between safeguarding the natural environment and meeting the various demands placed on the area by particular interests. Although only the periphery of the East Cairngorms has experienced the concentrated economic activity in the past, the scale and intensity of certain economic and recreational developments now require appropriate, sensitive controls.

A possible approach to securing the Plan's objectives would be the introduction of tiered zoning, with areas zoned according to their prime value or interest. The criteria and area of these zones would need to be clearly set out. At certain locations the opportunities to sustain the social and economic welfare of communities should be identified as an integral and important element of the Plan.

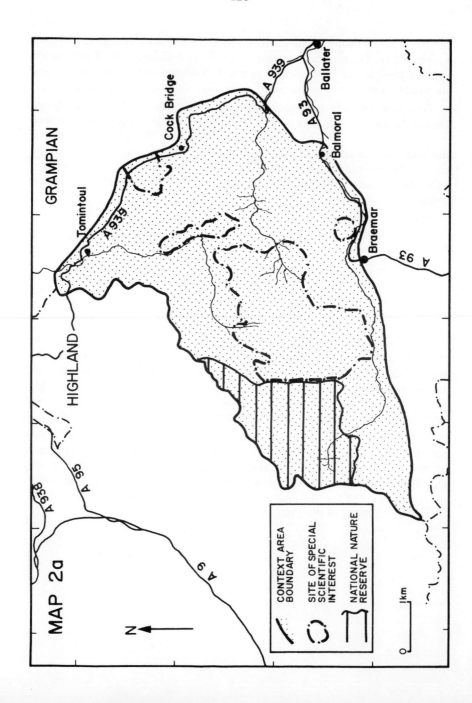

MAP 2a

N

GRAMPIAN

HIGHLAND

Tomintoul

Cock Bridge

Ballater

Balmoral

Braemar

A 939

A 939

A 93

A 93

A 9

A 95

A 938

CONTEXT AREA
BOUNDARY

SITE OF SPECIAL
SCIENTIFIC
INTEREST

NATIONAL NATURE
RESERVE

0   1km

127

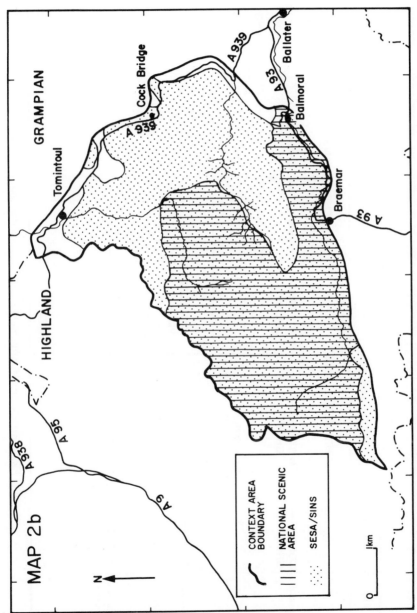

Maps 2a and 2b. The East Cairngorms management area showing current protective designations.

128

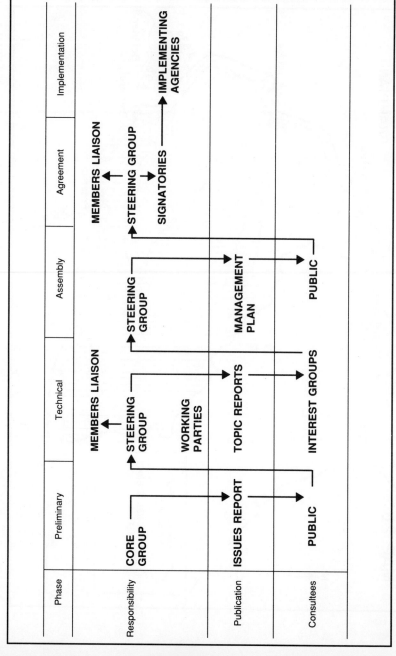

Table 1. East Cairngorms Management Plan: organisation and procedure

ORGANISATION AND PROCEDURE (Table 1)

The East Cairngorms Management Plan will be promoted by Grampian Regional Council. The inaugural meeting was in June 1988, by a Core Group of staff from Grampian Regional Council, District Councils, Nature Conservancy Council, and Countryside Commission for Scotland, with representatives from the Scottish Wildlife and Countryside Link and the Scottish Landowners Federation, and with the Scottish Development Department as an observer. The Core Group's task is to prepare an Issues Report which will be the subject of public consultation. This Report, which will be produced following brief initial work, will highlight some of the perceived conflicts, issues and possible mechanisms for their solution.

Its aim should not be to establish a co-ordinated approach by the Core Group but rather to state all views and to gather basic information on the natural environment, economy, proposed developments and pressures for change. This will not be an exhaustive study, being sufficient merely to illuminate broad issues and be capable of later refinement. To elicit a response from a wide cross-section of the public with an interest in the East Cairngorms, the Issues Report will be made widely available, not only at the normal local authority outlets, but also in climbing and ski shops, youth hostels etc. Currently, the members of the Core Group are preparing individual notes on how they perceive the main issues. The Issues Report will be available in 1990.

Following public consultation on the Issues Report, the Core Group will be expanded to become the Steering Group, consisting of officers and technical representatives. The exact composition of this Group has yet to be established. It is expected that in preparation and consultation of the Issues Report, appropriate individuals and organisations will be identified who can then be invited to join the Steering Group. The formation of Working Parties reporting to the Steering Group would allow specific details and problems to be examined such as red deer management and natural regeneration of native woodland.

The Steering Group will prepare the Management Plan after consultation and technical study. The purpose of consultation is to secure a high degree of confidence and trust between those preparing the plan and all interested parties, both private and public, who will be expected to implement and observe the proposals.

A draft Management Plan will be prepared indicating:

a. administrative context;

b. priorities for conservation;

c.   resource management priorities;

d.   development opportunities and constraints;

e.   planning strategy and control priorities;

f.   monitoring and review procedures.

Complementary to the Steering Group would be a Members' Liaison Committee comprised of members of local authorities along with Commissioners or officers of the Countryside Commission for Scotland and Nature Conservancy Council. The committee chairman should be a member of the Regional Council as regional planning authority.

CONSULTATION

The Issues Report and the draft Plan will be the subject of consultation with statutory bodies and with private and voluntary organisations with an interest in the East Cairngorms. Following responses to the draft, the East Cairngorms Management Plan will be published by Grampian Regional Council. It is hoped that it will not only be approved by the relevant statutory bodies but also be accepted by, and incorporated in the work of, a wide variety of private and voluntary organisations.

Public funds to assist with possible projects are potentially available from such bodies as the Countryside Commission for Scotland, the Scottish Sports Council and the Nature Conservancy Council. The Management Plan priorities should be reflected in any grants which are awarded and in improved co-ordination between the agencies concerned, both public and private.

It is intended that the final Plan will be available in 1991. The preparation of a Management Plan for the East Cairngorms is a good opportunity to lobby for new funding for the management of this outstanding area.

CONCLUSION

With increasing interest and investment in the East Cairngorms, potential conflicts between privately financed schemes (for estate management, recreation etc.) and public agencies and other bodies will inevitably develop. It is hoped that these can be resolved or reduced through early consultation and agreement. If not, at least they will be highlighted in the Management Plan as areas of potential difficulty.

The Regional Council is under no illusions as to the difficulty of reaching meaningful agreements on the complex and sensitive issues facing the area. The decision to embark upon the East Cairngorms Management Plan recognises that further designations to protect specific interests will not solve these wider problems. Instead, a solution is being sought from within the area, from those who have most to lose and most to contribute.

REFERENCES

GRAMPIAN REGIONAL COUNCIL (1984). *Grampian Region Part Structure Plan: Rural Area.* Grampian Regional Council, Aberdeen.

HMSO (1947). *National Parks and the Conservation of Nature (Scotland).* Cmnd Paper 7235. HMSO, London.

*FOOTNOTE. It should be noted that since the submission of the above paper the Government has asked the Countryside Commission for Scotland to study management arrangements for popular mountain areas such as the Cairngorms. The conclusions and recommendations arising from this work are to be reported to the Scottish Office during 1990. The work being promoted by Grampian Regional Council is regarded as an essential part of any management plan for the Eastern Cairngorms, irrespective of the eventual outcome of the review of the Management of Popular Mountain Areas.

PLANNING FOR DOWNHILL SKIING AT CAIRN GORM

H. BRINDLEY

Department of Planning, Highland Regional Council,
Glenurquhart Road, Inverness IV3 5NX

SUMMARY

1. This paper concentrates on the Cairngorm skiing centre and describes what has been happening since the Lurcher's Gully Public Inquiry in 1981.

2. National Planning Guidelines were produced by the Scottish Development Department in 1984 as a result of that Inquiry, and these identify the Cairngorm centre as a primary Scottish skiing area. The Nature Conservancy Council designated the Northern Corries of Cairn Gorm as a Site of Special Scientific Interest in 1984, partly as a result of the findings of the Public Inquiry. The Highlands and Islands Development Board has prepared a Management Plan for its Cairngorm Estate and has appointed George Stewart to co-ordinate management with all interested parties. This is the first management initiative of this kind on a large Scottish upland estate. The Countryside Commission for Scotland and Highland Regional Council have jointly prepared a Handbook on Environmental Design and Management in Ski Areas.

3. This paper assesses demand for downhill skiing and its potential growth over the next few years and looks at the capacity of existing and new skiing centres to cope. It goes on to describe the findings of the Highland Regional Council's Working Party on Development at Cairn Gorm. These findings are incorporated in the Council's Structure Plan which was publicised for comment in December 1988. Briefly the policies require:

    a. consolidation as a first phase within Coire Cas and Coire na Ciste and into Coire Laogh Mor to the east;

    b. a second phase of expansion into Lurcher's Gully by means of a private service road;

    c. no artefacts inside Coire an t-Sneachda and Coire an Lochain;

    d. a full environmental assessment of this second phase before any planning application is considered;

    e. the preparation of a Management Plan for the Cairn Gorm area;

    f. the setting up of an Advisory/Monitoring Group for future management of the Cairn Gorm area including the ski area, Forestry Commission area, Rothiemurchus Estate and that part of the NNR which lies within Highland Region.

INTRODUCTION

When one looks back at the history of events affecting the Cairngorms in the last forty years, the development of downhill skiing has been a major theme. Downhill skiing began in Scotland before the Second World War (Simpson 1982), but it was not until the late 1950s and early 1960s that mechanised commercial uplift skiing began to expand. Its growth in popularity since then has been rapid in Scotland and many other countries.

THE LURCHER'S GULLY PUBLIC INQUIRY

In this paper I concentrate on the Cairn Gorm ski centre. I start not at the beginning of skiing at Cairn Gorm but at 1981 when the first major public debate about skiing here took place. The history of this event, the Lurcher's Gully Public Inquiry, is well known, but is still worth a brief description (Scottish Development Department 1982a). The planning application by the Cairngorm Chairlift Company Ltd. in 1981 was to extend uplift facilities and comprised a road extension and new car park at the bottom of Allt Creag an Leth-choin (Lurcher's Gully), two new chairlifts, and new ski tows extending into Coire an t-Sneachda, Coire an Lochain, and Lurcher's Gully (Map 1). The Lurcher's Gully Public Inquiry ran from May to October 1981, and in December 1982 the Secretary of State refused planning permission. In his decision letter (Scottish Development Department 1982b) he emphasised that he did not intend his decision to rule out the possibility of a more limited scheme for additional facilities at Cairn Gorm, and that such a scheme which required no road extension beyond the existing car park might represent an acceptable balance between development and conservation objectives.

EVENTS FOLLOWING THE LURCHER'S GULLY PUBLIC INQUIRY

In January 1984 the Secretary of State published his *National Planning Guidelines for Skiing Developments* (Scottish Development Department 1984). These regarded Cairn Gorm as a primary area in Scotland. The Guidelines state:

> The improvement and expansion of facilities in this established centre in the central sector should be a priority aim, with a presumption in favour of developments within Coire Cas and Coire na Ciste, and expansion into areas with skiing potential outwith the National Nature Reserve. In preparing development schemes full account should be taken of the general principles and there should be a presumption against road

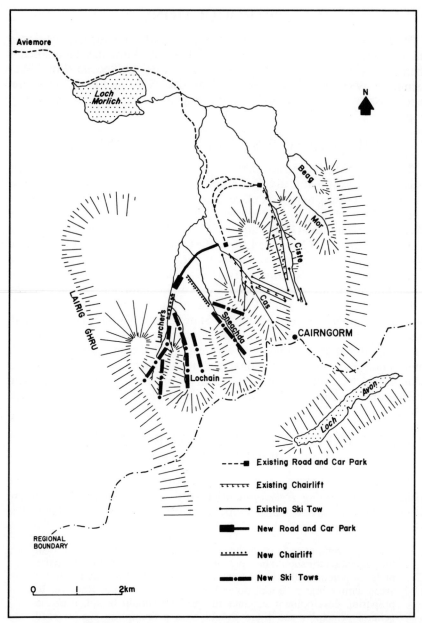

Map 1. The Northern Corries: The 1981 planning application.

extensions beyond the present car parks and any developments other than snow fencing within Coire an t-Sneachda and Coire an Lochain.

Also in 1984, the Nature Conservancy Council (NCC) designated the Northern Corries (Coire an t-Sneachda, Coire an Lochain and Allt Creag an Leth-choin) as a Site of Special Scientific Interest (Map 2). The area is described as an integral part of the internationally important Cairngorms massif. The variety of physical and biological features which they contain make them the most valuable of all the arctic-alpine cliff corries within the Cairngorms. The site contains one of the finest assemblages of glacial, fluvioglacial, periglacial landforms and erosion surfaces in Britain and other parts of Europe. The plant communities are also special, with some of the best cliff and scree flora in the Cairngorms to be found higher up in the magnificent cliff buttresses, ridges and deeply indented gullies. The lower slopes are predominantly covered by heather and deer sedge, whilst on the upper slopes snow and wind related vegetation is characterised by extensive areas of woolly hair moss, bearberry, and rush. Native Scots pine and juniper are becoming re-established on the lower slopes because of a big reduction in red deer grazing.

In June 1985, the Highlands and Islands Development Board (HIDB) published its draft *Cairngorm Estate Management Plan* (Highland and Islands Development Board 1987). This was subject to wide consultation with interested parties and was adopted in August 1987. Its aim was to further the development of the recreation and sporting opportunities offered by the Board's Cairngorm Estate, while ensuring that adverse impacts on scenery, plant and animal communities, soils, and geological and geomorphological features in and around the Estate be kept to a minimum. It stated ten objectives which will be pursued in the management of the Estate. Now that the Management Plan has been adopted, the HIDB has appointed George Stewart as co-ordinator to pursue its principles and proposals.

The HIDB sponsored research during the 1980s to provide a better understanding of the demand for skiing in Scotland, and also to assess the contribution that skiing makes to the economy of the Highlands (Mackay Consultants 1986, 1988). Table 1 shows the growth in demand for skiing in Scotland in terms of total skier days. These studies showed that between two and a half and three million people in Britain have gone skiing, with regular skiers numbering half a million. In 1985/86 it was estimated that skiing generated about £10 million of income in Strath Spey, equivalent to about 280 full-time jobs (Mackay Consultants 1986).

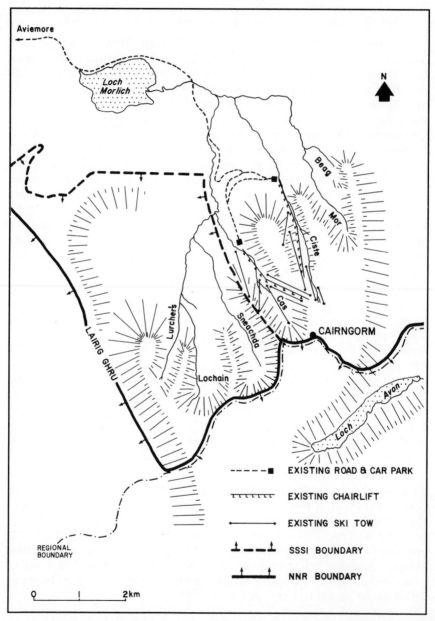

Map 2. The Northern Corries SSSI and the Cairngorms NNR.

	1978/79	1985/86	1986/87
Cairngorm	215 000	350 000	360 000
Glenshee	95 000	180 000	225 000
Glencoe	25 000	6 000	23 000
Lecht	–	63 000	95 000

Table 1. The number of skier days at the different ski resorts in Scotland (data from Mackay Consultants 1988 per annum)

In December 1985, the Countryside Commission for Scotland (CCS) and Highland Regional Council jointly published a report entitled *Environmental Design and Management of Ski Areas in Scotland. A Practical Handbook* (ASH Environmental Design Partnership 1986). The purpose of this handbook is to promote good standards of design and environmental management in ski areas in Scotland. It is intended to provide sound advice about the development of downhill ski areas in ways which strive to retain the natural beauty of the upland landscape as far as possible, while enabling the sport to be run effectively. The report recommended the establishment of development and management plans for all centres, including schemes for monitoring and assessing the impacts of ski facilities on the environment.

During this period, significant developments were taking place in other skiing centres in Scotland. Although not central to this paper, they are of interest.

1. Planning permissions were granted for new skiing centres at Jean's Gully, Drumochter and Dalwhinnie Corries. The former has not progressed because the landowner prefers to see the first development on the estate at Dalwhinnie. A lease has now been concluded for this latter site and the promoters are confident that they can secure private capital for the development. This proposal has an initial capacity to handle 40 000 skier days per annum, mainly intermediate skiers. It comprises a private road access from a car park next to the A9 to the 610 metres level, and three ski tows.

2. The proposed development at Aonach Mor near Fort William is now on course after difficulties in securing sufficient private capital to meet the Government's requirements for public funds. The capacity of this proposal, taking account of the poorer weather on the west coast (heavy precipitation and low cloud), is estimated to be initially 75 000 skier days per annum. A gondola access will be provided from a low-level car park to 610 metres, and a chairlift and three ski tows will extend into Snow Goose Gully. Direct

employment from this scheme will be fifty jobs with 100 to 130 downstream jobs in Fort William.

3.   Glenshee, where the Cairnwell chairlift opened in 1962, now has two chairlifts and sixteen tows. Permission was granted by the Secretary of State for the Glas Maol tow in 1986. A development and management plan for the Centre has been agreed by Kincardine and Deeside District Council, with significant prospects for extending the uplift capacity (Glenshee Chairlift Company 1987). The leased area at Glenshee has the largest uplift capacity of any Scottish skiing centre at present. An environmental baseline study has been produced (Watson 1988) and Dr Adam Watson has reported annually on environmental management measures since 1986.

4.   At the Lecht centre alongside the A939, six tows have now been installed, in the Ladder Hills SSSI. A development and management plan for Moray and Gordon District Council was updated in 1988 (Lecht Ski Company 1988). Since 1984, Dr Adam Watson has been carrying out environmental monitoring annually.

OVERALL FORECASTS OF DEMAND

That demand will continue to rise rapidly appears no longer to be disputed. On the basis of recent trends, a realistic minimum estimate of the pressure for growth in Scottish skiing is an average of five per cent per annum for the next five years. This would result in a net increase of almost 200 000 skier days, and a total of 902 000 skier days per annum by 1991-92. On the other hand if the actual average annual rate of growth for the past five years (fifteen per cent) were to continue, demand in future would rise to 1 400 000 skier days per annum by 1991-92.

The actual rate of growth could be substantially greater than five per cent. Skiing in Scotland is supply led. The lack of facilities and constraints on slope capacity at centres presently operating could be suppressing demand. As many as fifteen per cent of Scottish skiers are thought not to ski regularly. Mackay (1988) suggests that growth could increase by up to 300 000 skier days per annum by 1991-92 if the potential for expansion at existing centres is realised (accommodating an additional 215 000-265 000 skier days per annum) and new centres (with capacity for an additional 115 000 skier days per annum) begin to operate.

A DEVELOPMENT PLAN: SKIING AT CAIRNGORM

In March 1986, The Cairngorm Chairlift Company Ltd. produced its own development plan for the 1990s (Cairngorm Chairlift Company 1986). This accompanied a planning application to erect snow fencing on the west-side of Fiacaill a' Choire Chais for a more regular link to the snow fields of Coire an t-Sneachda, which was approved by the Regional Council. The Regional Council also decided to set up a Working Group with the Cairngorm Chairlift Company, HIDB, NCC and CCS to assess this development plan.

As a first step an Advisory Team was established. Its remit was:

a. to assess the Company's plan;

b. to assist the Director of Planning to prepare a framework for the development, improvement, conservation and phasing of the area;

and in so doing

c. to take account of other key fields of activity at Cairn Gorm and the potential impact of development on surrounding land.

The Team was not expected to initiate major new surveys, nor to agree on all issues. Its primary role was advisory.

The Team met on six occasions during the first half of 1987. From the outset the Team's composition was contentious, because it was decided not to include representatives of the voluntary organisations and groups with a keen interest in the Cairngorms. This was a deliberate policy in order to keep the Team small and manageable. The Issues Paper produced by the Team after its first three meetings, and its final report were widely circulated for comment, but there continues to be criticism that voluntary bodies should have been involved in the meetings.

The Advisory Team's Report was presented to the working Group in September 1987. The Team had reached agreement on a number of points, particularly;

a. that pressure of demand for skiing will continue, and Cairn Gorm is faced with the prospect of trying to accommodate an additional 100 000 skier days per annum by the early 1990s;

b. that consolidation within the existing centre and to the east is possible and should be pursued immediately;

and

c. that the ambience inside the two spectacular corries to the West – Coire an t-Sneachda and Coire an Lochain – should be maintained by keeping them free of artefacts except for limited snow fencing.

The representatives from NCC could not accept a carefully sited and managed development at Lurcher's Gully, which would avoid the key features of scientific interest in the area. They argued that the site's importance lies not so much in any one of its key features but as a complete unit of territory with an interlinked mosaic of communities and habitats, none of which should be disturbed.

The Advisory Team produced a Framework Plan, suggesting a form of development in the SSSI which would meet its remit (Map 3). The NCC officials did not accept this Plan and advised that no development should take place beyond the consolidation of the existing facilities in Coire na Ciste and Coire Cas and expansion into the corries in the east.

A key feature of the Framework Plan is a private road for a shuttle bus service run by the Chairlift Company as a means of access to Lurcher's Gully. The Team felt that this was preferable to ski tows or chairlifts which would have more visual impact and would be less adaptable for day to day management, evacuation etc. The Team also decided that a service building should be provided at the end of this private road.

The Working Group met twice to consider this report. At its first meeting it was agreed to seek written observations from voluntary organisations, and to commission a feasibility and cost study of the private road. Its final conclusions, which have now been agreed by Highland Regional Council, were:

1. demand for skiing at Cairn Gorm is expected to continue to increase, despite development at other existing and new centres elsewhere.

2. Consolidation within and east of the existing skiing area should be pursued as a matter of priority.

3. Such consolidation will ease but not solve the growing pressure of demand.

4. Measures to restrict the numbers of skiers at Cairn Gorm will be difficult to achieve, and according to local tourist organisations, ski schools and the Cairngorm Chairlift Company, unless capacity is increased, dissatisfaction with the centre will grow, diminishing the reputation of Strath Spey and Scottish skiing as a whole. However, some way to limit the numbers of skiers who use the resort may be necessary for the future, and possible measures must therefore be investigated by the Chairlift Company and the Highland and Islands Development Board. (In the Nature Conservancy Council's view, some such measures are necessary now in the interests of the safety and enjoyment of skiers). There are no statistical or market opinion survey data to show the levels of dissatisfaction. However the Advisory Team interviewed a number of parties, including representatives of the local tourist trade, ski schools and skiers' associations, and all these were concerned about queueing at tows and lifts, congestion on the slopes, and increase in collision accidents.

The Cairngorm ski centre is not like other recreational or cultural facilities where the doors can be closed when the stadium or hall is full. We

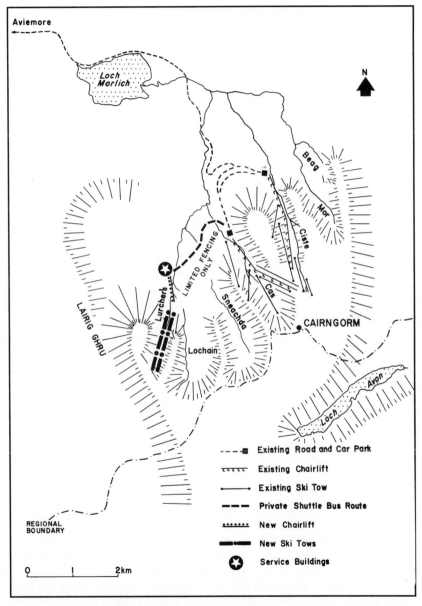

Map 3. Cairngorm Development Plan advisory team suggestion for development in the SSSI.

cannot turn people away at Glen More if the capacity for the day has been reached or if they do not have a ticket. The road is a public one and access to the Cairngorms is open to walkers, cross-country skiers and others. The only reason for closing the public road is bad weather and safety. That is why we say that measures to restrict downhill skiers will be difficult to achieve. The measures which the Working Group wishes to be investigated are:

   a. advance information about the capacity of the day;

   b. investigation of ticket systems to regulate numbers at peak days;

   c. car parking capacity controls.

5.   The visual impact of a carefully sited skiing development at Lurcher's Gully can be limited to a localised area. This should not materially detract from views from the Cairn Gorm plateau rim or from Loch Morlich and the A9.

6.   The special ambience typified by the solitude and enclosed grandeur of the inner Northern Corries (which begins to be experienced above altitudes of approximately 910 metres in Coire an t-Sneachda and 880 metres in Coire an Lochain) can be maintained, provided that further snow fencing on the foreground of the corries and adjoining ridges avoids skylining and is limited to short stretches required to link up the main snow fields, and provided that other artefacts are absent.

7.   The key landforms and rare plant communities of the Northern Corries SSSI should not be impaired by a carefully sited and managed skiing development. (Whilst accepting that these features, above the potential development area would not be directly affected, they represent, in the Nature Conservancy Council's view, only a part of the SSSI's interest. The NCC stress that the national significance of the SSSI depends on maintaining the site in its entirety as a whole ecological unit, which includes the altitudinal range of plant communities from plateau to closed pine wood. In NCC's view, mechanised skiing would seriously damage this scientific interest and the intrusive nature of development would also detract from the appreciation of the natural interest by visitors).

8.   Access to Lurcher's Gully should be provided by a private shuttle bus service on a road dedicated to that service and essential maintenance requirements, and prohibited to other vehicles. If this is contrary to the National Planning Guidelines and not acceptable to the Secretary of State, a chairlift or other cable system would provide adequate access for skiers and maintenance needs. Given (7) above, this conclusion is not accepted by the Nature Conservancy Council nor the Countryside Commission for Scotland (Countryside Commission for Scotland 1989).

9. The advisory/monitoring group comprising representatives of the main interested bodies should be convened by the Highlands and Islands Development Board to advise on future management of the area.

10. Consolidation within Coire Cas and Coire na Ciste, and further east (principally into Coire Laogh Mor) should be undertaken as a first phase. Subject to suitable technical and financial assessment this is likely to comprise:

  a. alterations to the lower chairlift in Coire na Ciste to take beginners to the middle station and open up more nursery areas:

  b. a new tow in upper Coire na Ciste on to the flank of Cairn Gorm to open up higher snowfields and make Coire Laogh Mor more easily skiable when conditions are suitable;

  c. new snow fencing to consolidate runs in upper Coire Laogh Mor to allow return to the uplift in Coire na Ciste;

  and

  d. lower uplift to link Coire Cas and Coire na Ciste.

11. expansion into Lurcher's Gully as a separate phase should comprise the following options for consideration:

  a. a double tow on the east flank of Lurcher's, starting at approximately 700 metres altitude;

  b. one building for shelter, refreshments and essential operational needs, located at the bottom of Lurcher's Gully at approximately 650 metres altitude;

  c. a chairlift linking (a) and (b) above;

  d. restricted snow fencing across the foreground of Coire an t-Sneachda and Coire an Lochain, limited to that required to link the main snow holding pockets and to allow skiing back to Coire Cas when there is good snow cover. Below the corries' foreground, snow fencing would be required to consolidate beginners' areas in a few places;

  e. all artefacts, buildings and pistes to be located well clear of the key features of scientific interest, namely the rare plant communities and glacial landforms;

  f. construction and management measures would be designed to minimise erosion, although patches of localised erosion would require reseeding in small areas;

  g. a preferred means of access based upon a private service road linking the car park at Coire Cas and the building at (b) above. This would probably follow one of the alternative alignments identified in the feasibility study prepared by Highland Regional Council's Regional Roads Unit in November 1987, and the design and construction criteria therein.

THE FUTURE

The Chairlift Company and HIDB have commissioned consultants to undertake a detailed environmental assessment of the suggestions of the Advisory Team. This assessment is now available and forms one of the background papers to the Regional Council's Structure Plan Review (Highland Regional Council 1988). This Review contains policies for development at Cairn Gorm based on the conclusions of the Working Group. The Structure Plan Draft has been subject to wide consultation during the Spring of 1989. Over 5000 letters of representation have been received on the Cairn Gorm policies, fairly evenly balanced between those in favour and those opposed. The Regional Council has considered these representations carefully but is expected to confirm its Structure Plan policies for Cairn Gorm and to forward the Plan to the Secretary of State during the Autumn of 1989.

Is another Public Inquiry on the cards? Opposition to the extension of facilities towards Lurchers Gully is strong from conservation and recreational organisations. Indeed the Countryside Commission for Scotland, after long deliberation, has determined to oppose expansion in the form suggested in the draft Structure Plan (Countryside Commission for Scotland 1989). It still remains to be seen whether the Secretary of State will choose another long and expensive Inquiry to help him reach a decision.

REFERENCES

ASH ENVIRONMENTAL DESIGN PARTNERSHIP (1986). *Environmental Design of Ski Areas in Scotland. A Practical Handbook.* Report for the Countryside Commission for Scotland and Highland Regional Council. ASH Environmental Design Partnership, Glasgow.

CAIRNGORM CHAIRLIFT COMPANY (1986). *Development Plan for the 1980s and 1990s.* Cairngorm Chairlift Company, Inverness.

COUNTRYSIDE COMMISSION FOR SCOTLAND (1989). *Westward Expansion of Skiing at Cairngorm.* Countryside Commission for Scotland, Perth.

GLENSHEE CHAIRLIFT COMPANY (1987). *Development and Management Plan for Glenshee Ski Centre 1987-1991.* Glenshee Chairlift Company, Braemar.

HIGHLANDS AND ISLANDS DEVELOPMENT BOARD (1987). *Cairngorm Estate Management Plan.* Highlands and Islands Development Board, Inverness.

HIGHLAND REGIONAL COUNCIL (1988). *Highland Region Structure Plan Review 1988* (Consultative Draft), Highland Regional Council.

LECHT SKI COMPANY (1988). *Development and Management Plan.* Lecht Ski Company, Strathdon.

MACKAY CONSULTANTS (1986). *Expenditure of Skiers at Cairngorm and Glencoe.* Highlands and Islands Development Board, Inverness.

MACKAY CONSULTANTS (1988). *The Future Development of the Scottish Skiing Industry.* Scottish Development Agency, Edinburgh.

SCOTTISH DEVELOPMENT DEPARTMENT (1982a). *Findings of the Lurcher's Gully Public Inquiry, Kingussie.* Scottish Development Department, Edinburgh.

SCOTTISH DEVELOPMENT DEPARTMENT (1982b). *Lurcher's Gully Public Inquiry – Decision Letter.* Scottish Development Department, Edinburgh.

SCOTTISH DEVELOPMENT DEPARTMENT, (1984) *National Planning Guidelines for Skiing Developments.* Scottish Development Department, Edinburgh.

SIMPSON, M. (1982). *Skisters: the Story of Scottish Skiing.* Landmark, Carrbridge.

WATSON, A. (1988). *Environmental Baseline Study – Glenshee Ski Centre 1987.* Institute of Terrestrial Ecology, Banchory.

AN ASSESSMENT OF THE LANDSCAPE AND SCENIC QUALITY OF THE CAIRNGORMS

DAVID RICE

Countryside Commission for Scotland, Battleby, Redgorton, Perth PH1 3EW

SUMMARY

1.   The Cairngorms plateau is one of the best known mountain areas in Britain. It affords opportunity for a wide range of recreational activity, participants being drawn to the area by its important scenic quality. This quality has been recognised for many years and the area was listed in 1981 by the Countryside Commission for Scotland as a National Scenic Area.

2.   The dramatic and bold landscape character of the mountain plateau is enhanced by surrounding native pine woodlands and straths containing a variety of vegetation, land-use and scenic character.

3.   Man's influence on the landscape has resulted in the loss of the Old Caledonian pine woods, the introduction of development, particularly downhill skiing, on the northern side of the massif and artefacts and man-induced changes to the inner heartland of the wild Cairngorms.

4.   This national landscape asset deserves careful conservation and sensitive management for the existing and anticipated demands for the range of outdoor recreation pursuits which exist.

INTRODUCTION

The Cairngorms plateau contains landscapes of national significance and together with its surrounding straths and glens presents a great variety of highland scenery that is deserving of careful conservation, as well as presenting a range of opportunities for informal countryside recreation which increasingly require sensitive management.

The Cairngorms are the highest part of a large mountain area in the central Highlands of Scotland. Although this area is dominated by metamorphic rock, the Cairngorms and Lochnagar plateaux are comprised of important intrusions of granite. Situated on the southeast side of the River Spey, the Cairngorms consist of a bold, rounded, granite plateau. The smooth, rounded summit areas of the Cairngorms are broken only by rock tors, although deep troughs and corries were cut by glaciation into the upper surface of the plateau. The Lairig Ghru and Lairig an Laoigh are narrow, steep-sided cuts through the Cairngorms massif. This is a nationally important area where the vast corries, the massive slopes, the long passes, the wide skies and the very bareness of the ground, where the elements work with a power not known at lower altitudes, give these plateaux their distinctive quality (Murray 1962).

The mountain massif has physical characteristics not found in other parts of the Highlands or Britain. It includes the most extensive area of land over 1000 metres and has four of the five highest hills in Britain. Ben Macdui, Braeriach, Cairn Toul and Cairn Gorm are all over 1200 metres. Other well-known summits are Beinn a' Bhuird, Ben Avon and Cairn Lochan. The national importance of the area has long been recognised. It was a National Park Direction Area (NPDA) until 1981, when that designation was replaced by National Scenic Area status. The Cairngorms was one of the three areas suggested by the Countryside Commission for Scotland in its report *A Park System for Scotland* as being suitable for consideration as a special park (Countryside Commission for Scotland 1974). The grandeur and ruggedness of this area combine to produce one of Scotland's foremost areas for mountain recreation.

The height of the Cairngorms is less immediately apparent than the bulk of the massif. On the plateau the views are vast and the immensity of space and scale are impressive. The edges of the plateau are glacially sculpted into huge corries which excel in grandeur anything to be found elsewhere in Scotland, with the possible exception of Coire Leis on Ben Nevis. Where the plateau edge is not etched by corries, there are long, smooth, steep slopes which, seen from Speyside, rise in tiers (Countryside Commission for Scotland 1978). Snow lies for a long time at the top of these slopes, and lifts and other facilities for downhill skiing have been developed in Coire Cas and Coire na Ciste.

THE STRATHS AND GLENS

Lower down these slopes, deer forest, sheep grazing and forestry assume greater importance in the appearance of the landscape. It is the surrounding forests which for many people characterise the Cairngorms. Within Strath Spey are extensive remnants of the native Caledonian pine forest at Rothiemurchus, Abernethy and Glen Feshie. These wooded flanks of the Cairngorms form a setting of rare beauty for the mountain massif and are in turn enhanced by the mountain backdrop.

The strath of the River Spey contains a great variety of vegetation, land-use and scenic character. The mountains are set back from the river, creating space for other features of interest, yet are never so far removed as not to present an important backdrop in the views. The valley bottom comprises a mixture of lush meadows, arable land, marshland, lochs and woodland. The scene is full of variety, at one moment enclosed intimately with deciduous woodland and gentle undulations, the next in open ground with vistas across lochs to impressive mountainsides and the mouths of tributary glens. On Rothiemurchus Estate, for example, the pines on the upper forest slopes give way to a mixture of pine and birch, and then to the rich policy woodlands close by the River Spey. The pine forests are deeply carpeted with heather, blaeberry and other forest understorey plants, and the woods are interspersed with lochans of varying character, with views culminating in the waters of the Spey itself. Across the steeper hillsides and along the edge of river terraces are large areas of birch woodland, where natural regeneration is frequently poor because of browsing pressure. Farms and estate boundaries usually run from the river banks up the hillsides to the ridges, so that each holding has a share of the better land in the valley bottom. Large-scale intensive afforestation has occurred at places such as Inshriach, Glen More and Kinveachy, but the over-riding woodland scene is of native pine woodland and individual 'granny' Scots pines.

In contrast to the strath of the Spey, the landscape of Glen Feshie is wilder and sterner, and the pines mature and more scattered, interspersed with juniper. The river dominates this forest, a great, braided mountain stream with shingle beds cast over an uneven flood plain, almost continental in scale.

Mar Forest, to the east of the plateau, differs yet again. Higher, and therefore less rich than Rothiemurchus in its flora, it graduates from birch, through to massive ancient pines and birch again with a ground cover of heather and blaeberry. Like Glen Feshie, the rivers here are important too, but not for their scale and grandeur – they are noisy burns, dashing over boulders of granite and mica schist washed brightly pink and silvery by their clear waters, a lively element in the landscape.

The character of Deeside is epitomised by the steep enclosing wooded valley sides, by frequent views of the river, and the unfolding of a new scene around each bend of the valley. Upstream of Braemar, the valley has been widened and straightened by late glacial action. The Lui and Quoich waters enter the valley from narrow enclosed glens which afford walkers fine approaches to the Cairngorms massif. The flood-plain narrows at the Linn of Dee where the river thunders through narrow rock-cuts and cauldrons. The valley floor has a little pastoral agriculture, and there are fine stretches of pine and birch woods, and stands of old Norway spruce and larch that reach up the side glens. Coniferous afforestation has added to the natural woodland and there are also planted broadleaved species in the many estate policies in the valley. Ballochbuie Forest is a superb example of Old

Caledonian pine woodland, the beauty of which impressed Queen Victoria, who purchased it to remove the threat of felling. The relationship of the fine woodland, with its understorey of heather and blaeberry, to the river and the flanks of Lochnagar form a beautiful landscape. In upper Deeside the scenery along most of the river has been further varied by the influences which Queen Victoria set in train. This is partly a managed cultural landscape in which castles, large houses and their planted policies complement the natural character. It is this combination of intrinsic beauty and cultural elements which makes Royal Deeside famous.

THE INFLUENCE OF MAN

Recent changes to the appearance of the Cairngorms may be classified under three broad headings. First, loss of the Caledonian pinewoods and their replanting using exotic species and modern forestry practices; second, the developments on the northern side of the massif that have followed from the opening of the area for a downhill skiing resort and intensive use for informal recreation; and third, the man-induced changes caused to the inner heartland of the wild Cairngorms.

FORESTRY AND THE OLD
CALEDONIAN PINE FOREST

Glen More Forest is one of the recognised native pinewoods, but it is perhaps the most modified of all. It was originally owned by the Dukes of Gordon. Major fellings were undertaken between 1783 and 1805. There followed a period of regeneration which lasted until 1916 when the timber was sold to the nation and felling was undertaken by the Canadian Forestry Corps. Felling was initially in the western forest around the Slugan Pass, and later in the Pass of Ryvoan and to the south of Loch Morlich. Around 126,000 trees were felled, scattered trees being left for regeneration. The size of this operation implies that there was probably a fairly open forest at the time of the felling.

The then new Forestry Commission purchased the estate in 1923 from the Duke of Richmond and Gordon. The forest was then largely re-stocked with exotic species, mainly Sitka spruce and Scots pine of mostly imported provenance, with lesser amounts of Norway spruce, lodgepole pine and larch. Very little felling of the Forestry Commission's plantings has taken place so far and only a small amount is planned up to the year 2000. In large part this reflects long rotations, due to the high altitude and infertility of the area, but trees have grown very poorly over some parts of the forest, particularly to the east and south of Loch Morlich, where many trees are in check.

Only two small sections of forest to the east of Loch Morlich can be considered as being pure Caledonian pine, the larger of which in Ryvoan Pass is managed as a reserve by the Scottish Wildlife Trust.

Generally, Glen More is a dull forest, as it is still mainly in first rotation. Suggestions have been made that it should be managed for return to a more native woodland. The coincidence of the main residual area of original pine and of poor forest growth could provide a lead to this idea, particularly as it is this land – to the south and east of Loch Morlich – that forms the forest foreground to the main view on to the Northern Corries. The Forestry Commission intends in some forthcoming fellings to enclose and treat the ground to encourage natural regeneration.

DOWNHILL SKIING DEVELOPMENTS AND RECREATION

The changes caused by provision of downhill skiing facilities and mass tourism into the area have been profound. These are part of a general social and economic change in Britain and elsewhere in the developed world. Over twenty five years, Aviemore has been transformed from a small village to a town dominated by leisure developments, and the traditional land uses have given way to the present leisure economy. These economic and physical changes are paralleled by equally strong cultural and social change, with a local population being now overtaken by an incoming and partly migrant workforce.

There has been benefit to local employment from tourism and numerous visitors have enjoyed recreation in the area, but the essential natural qualities of the Aviemore/Glen More area have been impaired. In part this results from the urbanised appearance of Aviemore, with discordant building styles rarely in harmony with traditional forms or the natural setting. This clutter of development and signs has spread some way along the Glen More road, itself a modern engineered highway.

Developments on Cairn Gorm mountain present two faces. In winter the movement of tows and skiers and the patterns of snow and ice combine to create a scene in Coire Cas and Coire na Ciste which seems lively to many people. In summer, when masking snow cover disappears, the visual impression of the industrial-scale car parks, buildings, tows and fences is of a rather bruised landscape. However, it should be noted that the Cairngorm Chairlift Company has made efforts to repair earlier damage arising from less sensitive methods of ski-field construction.

MAN'S INFLUENCE IN THE HEARTLAND

Away from the downhill skiing centre, change to the inner core of the Cairngorms massif is still on a relatively small scale, but at the same time small changes here are more damaging. It is, however, important to note that the wild land core has been penetrated for more than a century, as the main existing estate track network is recorded on the first edition of the Ordnance Survey 1" maps.

Changes arising from public access include bridges, bothies, cairns, litter, paths and damage to soils and vegetation caused by the impact of human feet. For some people, the presence of many others impairs their perception of the solitude of the area. Some redress of these changes has arisen from demolition of the high-level bothies on the plateau.

In the core of the area perhaps the most regrettable changes come from the bulldozing of vehicle tracks, which offend by their ugly construction. Construction of bulldozed tracks is now subject to planning control under the procedures for Development Control in National Scenic Areas, but increased use of all-terrain vehicles poses a new threat of damage to vulnerable ground.

REFERENCES

COUNTRYSIDE COMMISSION FOR SCOTLAND (1974). *A Park System for Scotland.* Countryside Commission for Scotland, Perth.

COUNTRYSIDE COMMISSION FOR SCOTLAND (1978). *Scotland's Scenic Heritage.* Countryside Commission for Scotland, Perth.

MURRAY, W.H. (1962). *Highland Landscape: a Survey.* National Trust for Scotland, Edinburgh.

APPENDIX 1

Scientific names of species referred to in text

SHRUBS

Bearberry	Arctostaphylos uva-ursi
Blackthorn	Prunus spinosa
Blaeberry	Vaccinium myrtillus
Cotton grass	Eriophorum vaginatum
Deer sedge	Trichophorum caespitosum
Heather	Calluna vulgaris
Heath rush	Juncus squarrosus
Purple moor grass	Molinia caerulea
Woolly hair moss	Rhacomitrium lanuginosum

TREES

Aspen	Populus tremula
Birch	Betula spp
	B. pendula
	B. pubescens
Juniper	Juniperus communis
Larch	Larix decidua
Lodgepole pine	Pinus contorta
Norway spruce	Picea abies
Scots pine	Pinus sylvestris
Sitka spruce	Picea sitchensis

BIRDS

Common buzzard	Buteo buteo
Crow	Corvus corone
Dotterel	Charadrius morinellus
Golden eagle	Aquila chrysaetos
Gull	Larus spp
Hen harrier	Circus cyaneus
Osprey	Pandion haliaetus
Peregrine falcon	Falco peregrinus
Ptarmigan	Lagopus mutus
Red grouse	Lagopus lagopus scoticus
Red kite	Milvus milvus
Snow bunting	Plectrophenax nivalis

MAMMALS

Fox	Vulpes vulpes
Mountain hare	Lepus timidus
Pine marten	Martes martes
Polecat	Mustela putorius
Rabbit	Oryctolagus cuniculus
Red deer	Cervus elaphus
Reindeer	Rangifer tarandus
Roe Deer	Capreolus capreolus
Wild cat	Felis silvestris

APPENDIX 2

List of Abbreviations used in the text

C
CCC   – Cairngorm Chairlift Company Ltd.
CCS   – Countryside Commission for Scotland

E
EC   – European Community
ESA   – Environmentally Sensitive Areas

H
HIDB   – Highlands and Islands Development Board
HMSO   – His/Her Majesty's Stationery Office
HRC   – Highland Regional Council

I
ITE   – Institute of Terrestrial Ecology
IUCN   – International Union for the Conservation of Nature and Natural
          Resources

N
NCC   – Nature Conservancy Council
NCR   – Nature Conservation Review
NNR   – National Nature Reserve
NPDA   – National Park Direction Area
NRA   – Nature Reserve Agreement

R
RSPB   – Royal Society for the Protection of Birds

S
SDD   – Scottish Development Department
SESA   – Study of Environmentally Sensitive Areas
SINS   – Sites of Interest to Natural Science
SSSI   – Site of Special Scientific Interest

U
UNEP   – United Nations Environment Programme

BIOGRAPHICAL NOTES

R. BALHARRY. Dick Balharry joined the Red Deer Commission in 1959 as a stalker before moving to the then Nature Conservancy as warden at their Beinn Eighe National Nature Reserve in Wester Ross. In 1968 he became Chief Warden with responsibility for all the nature reserves in the North West Region of the Conservancy. He is now the Chief Warden for the Conservancy's North East Region, and in this capacity has responsibility for the wardening of the Cairngorms National Nature Reserve. He is widely travelled and a recognised authority on the wildlife of Scotland.

HOWARD BRINDLEY is a Geography graduate from Leicester University. He worked for Greater London Council for five years before moving to the Planning Department of Ross and Cromarty County Council. Since 1975, he has been Senior Depute Director of Planning for Highland Regional Council. Howard Brindley chaired the Advisory Team to the Highland Regional Council's Cairngorm Working Party and has been closely involved in the preparation of the Council's Structure Plan Policy for the Cairngorms area.

The Rt Hon ALICK BUCHANAN-SMITH MP was educated at Edinburgh Academy, Glenalmond, Pembroke College, Cambridge and Edinburgh University. He completed National Service in the Gordon Highlanders. He first stood for Parliament in 1959 in West Fife and was elected as Conservative MP for North Angus and Mearns in 1964 and successfully contested the new seat for Kincardine and Deeside following the redistribution in 1983. From 1969 to May 1970 Mr Buchanan-Smith was a Conservative Spokesman for Scotland. On the formation of the Conservative government in June 1970 he was appointed Parliamentary Under Secretary of State for Home Affairs and Agriculture at the Scottish Office. From 1974-76 he was Opposition Spokesman for Scotland. Mr Buchanan-Smith has been a Minister of State at the Ministry of Agriculture, Fisheries and Food and at the Department of Energy. He was made a Privy Councillor in 1981. His hobbies include hill walking and skiing.

J.W.H. CONROY. Jim Conroy is a member of the Institute of Terrestrial Ecology and is currently involved in otter research. Prior to joining ITE, he spent eleven years with the British Antarctic Survey. A native of Morayshire, he has known the Cairngorms for over twenty-five years as climber, naturalist and conservationist. During that time he has been involved in teaching and introducing people to the area and its wildlife.

RONALD D. CRAMOND, now retired, was, at the time of the Conference, Deputy Chairman of the Highlands and Islands Development Board (since

1983), with special responsibility for the islands, tourism, agriculture and land use. He has wide experience of Government in Scotland including Under Secretary (Agriculture) in the Department of Agriculture and Fisheries Scotland, during which time he was Scottish member of the UK Delegation to the Agricultural Council in Brussels. Previously, as Under Secretary (Planning) in the Scottish Development Department, he was involved in the introduction of regional reports and structure plans, and the introduction of the first series of National Planning Guidelines. He has been a Commissioner with the Countryside Commission for Scotland since 1988. Recreations include hill walking and golf.

PROFESSOR KAI CURRY-LINDAHL is a biologist from Sweden. Formerly Senior Adviser in ecology and conservation to the United Nations Environment Programme, he has worked for over forty years on wildlife ecology, international conservation, outdoor recreation and wilderness management. He has advised many governments on related problems, and is author of some eighty books on these topics. He has paid a number of visits to the Cairngorms, and assessed the international standing of British Nature Reserves and National Parks.

BASIL DUNLOP is a Chartered Forester with twenty-three years' experience working in the forests of the Cairngorms. As Chief Forester of the Seafield Strathspey Estates from 1965 to 1984, he was involved in the management of the Kinveachy and both sections of the Abernethy pinewoods which were then owned by the estate, and carried out experiments and trials on natural regeneration. Since 1984 he has been a self-employed consultant specialising in the conservation of the native pinewoods, and has completed comprehensive surveys of the Rothiemurchus, Ballochbuie, south and north Abernethy and Kinveachy pinewoods.

JOHN GRANT OF ROTHIEMURCHUS is the fourteenth member of his family to be Laird of the Estate. After leaving Gordonstoun he spent five years in industry, spent a year working on a farm in the Black Isle, and studied the HND course in agriculture at Aberdeen. He has managed Rothiemurchus since 1976 and the Estate is now involved in among other things, nature conservation, forestry, and day recreation for tourists. He is a past Chairman of the Scottish Recreational Land Association, the Highland Farming, Forestry, and Wild Life Advisory Group, and is a Director of the British Deer Producers' Society, Scot Trout Limited and the Cairngorm Recreation Trust.

A.R. GUNSON. Rod Gunson graduated in Geography from Reading University and carried out research at Lancaster University into Climatic

Change during the Ice Age. He lectured at St Andrews and Leeds Universities before taking up his present post in the Geography Department at Aberdeen University. His teaching and research interests are in vegetation history, environmental change and landscape evolution. He has a keen interest in adult education having taught for the Open University since 1975. He is currently Organiser for Continuing Education in Aberdeen University with responsibility for the Access Course and Part-time degrees. He has been Conference Organiser for the Centre for Scottish Studies since 1983.

E. MICHAEL MATTHEW has been Regional Officer with the Nature Conservancy Council's North East Region since 1975. Prior to joining the Nature Conservancy in 1964 was educated at Cambridge and McGill Universities and University College, London. In his current position he has been involved in the management of the Cairngorms National Nature Reserve and in ski developments at three sites within the North East Region.

DAVID RICE is a Chartered Town Planner with a qualification in Landscape Architecture. He has worked for the Countryside Commission for Scotland since 1972 and has held the post of Regional Planning officer (North Scotland) since 1981. His work involves him in the preparation of the Commission's advice on planning and recreation issues in the Highlands and he was a member of the team of staff which carried out the scenic survey leading to the listing of National Scenic Areas. He was the Commission's representative on the Highland Regional Council's Cairngorm Working Party.

DR ADAM WATSON is a scientist with the Institute of Terrestrial Ecology at Banchory. He was brought up in Aberdeenshire, and has known the Cairngorms since 1938 as a walker, naturalist, climber and skier. Dr Watson is the recognised authority on the Cairngorms, author of the Scottish Mountaineering Club's District Guide to the Cairngorms, co-author of The Cairngorms, and has written many other publications on the area, of which some ecological studies have become international classics.

R. DRENNAN WATSON is a biologist who has spent most of his professional life as a specialist adviser and lecturer in agriculture at the North of Scotland College of Agriculture and the University of Aberdeen. He is currently a self-employed consultant on environmental and land use issues. His knowledge of the Cairngorms as a walker, climber and naturalist spans nearly thirty years. Through this involvement he has developed a strong interest in the management of mountain areas, and the conservation

of natural resources which he has studied in Scotland and abroad. He was the
first Chairman of the North East Mountain Trust and is currently Chairman
of the Scottish Wildlife and Countryside Link.